EPIDEICTIC RHETORIC

Ashley and Peter Larkin Series in Greek and Roman Culture

EPIDEICTIC RHETORIC

Questioning the Stakes of Ancient Praise

LAURENT PERNOT

UNIVERSITY OF TEXAS PRESS
Austin

First edition, 2015
First paperback printing, 2016

♾ The paper used in this book meets the minimum
requirements of ANSI/NISO Z39.48-1992 (R1997)
(Permanence of Paper).

LIBRARY OF CONGRESS CATALOGING-IN-PUBLICATION DATA
Pernot, Laurent, author.
Epideictic rhetoric : questioning the stakes of ancient praise /
Laurent Pernot. — First edition.
pages cm — (Ashley and Peter Larkin series
in Greek and Roman culture)
Includes bibliographical references and index.
ISBN 978-0-292-76820-8 (cloth : alk. paper)
1. Rhetoric, Ancient. 2. Speeches, addresses, etc., Greek—
History and criticism. 3. Speeches, addresses, etc., Latin—
History and criticism. 4. Oratory, Ancient. 5. Praise in
literature. 6. Blame in literature. I. Title. II. Series:
Ashley and Peter Larkin series in Greek and Roman culture.
PA3038.P458 2015
808.00938—dc23 2014031690

ISBN 978-1-4773-1133-2, paperback

doi:10.7560/768208

CONTENTS

PREFACE

This [sc. epideictic oratory] is a form of literature which has relatively few admirers today, but if we are to understand the Greeks thoroughly it seems necessary to understand, if not to share, their love for it.

GEORGE KENNEDY,
THE ART OF PERSUASION IN GREECE, 153

I have done a lot of work on epideictic throughout my life, from a two-volume book in French entitled *La rhétorique de l'éloge dans le monde gréco-romain* (The rhetoric of praise in the Greco-Roman world) to more recent papers. Yet I must confess that after decades of research, this topic still seems to possess difficult and puzzling aspects.

Everyone who studies this material knows that epideictic oratory represents in theory a third of all rhetoric (epideictic is one of three genres, along with judicial or forensic rhetoric and deliberative rhetoric). Scholars of rhetoric also know that epideictic oratory includes speeches of praise and blame, which are an important feature of practical speaking. But as soon as one moves beyond these elementary observations, questions arise, two in particular: one relates to the history of epideictic rhetoric, and the other to its function. From the historical point of view, epideictic developed differently from the two other genres. It was the least important of the three at the beginning of Greek oratory, but its role grew exponentially in subsequent periods. This historical development, which could not have been predicted, deserves an explanation. At the same time, while epideictic is important, its role remains unclear. Unlike judicial and deliberative speeches, epideictic orations are not meant to elicit any vote or any decision on the part of the listener. From a functional point of view, one is right to wonder what use they were.

Furthermore, in ancient and modern languages, "epideictic rhetoric" corresponds to a plurality of terms, a situation which may create confusion: for example, in English, we have "praise," "eulogy," "encomium," and "panegyric." Thus, "epideictic" raises some interpretative difficulties. It is therefore necessary to clarify, and to understand, this concept. The present book is intended to propose some answers; its focus is Greco-Roman antiquity, but the hope is that certain observations will be transferable to other periods, at least in part, and can contribute to the interpretation of epideictic in medieval, modern, and contemporary contexts. The Greek Classical period (fifth to fourth century BC) and the Roman Imperial period (first to fourth century AD) were brilliant and creative times in the history of epideictic rhetoric, and this is the reason they deserve our attention.

Because of the difficulties it raises, epideictic rhetoric is not an area researchers have explored very frequently. The last comprehensive treatment in English is T. Burgess's "Epideictic Literature" (diss., Chicago, 1902). This work, which was original for its time, had the advantage of seeing the subject in its largest extension, from the Classical period to the end of antiquity, taking into consideration both the theory and the practice of rhetoric and presenting a wide collection of references. However, Burgess defined "epideictic" too widely, including within it a large number of genres and literary forms, such as military addresses, philosophical works, diatribes, exhortations, and sermons, which had the effect of diluting the precise object of the research. The very title of his work is significant, as it is called "Epideictic Literature" and not "Epideictic Rhetoric."

Today there is a growing interest in this field. Several studies published in recent decades, each adopting different methods and subjects, show a tendency to take the function of epideictic speeches seriously, for example, concerning classical Greek funeral oration (Loraux 1986), the Latin panegyrics (MacCormack 1981), and Greek rhetoric of the fourth century AD and the Byzantine period (Kennedy 1983). Some recent collections of papers deal with both general issues (Urso 2011) and circumscribed corpora (Rees 2012; Roche 2011; Smith and Covino 2010).

The concept of "epideictic" plays a central part in J. Walker's *Rhetoric and Poetics in Antiquity* (2000). This important work transcends the boundaries between rhetoric and poetry and proposes an in-depth analysis of the functions of literature. Although Walker's approach is basically different from that of the present book, there is substantial compatibility, I think, between the two arguments, insofar as epideictic is recognized by both as a major phenomenon and a source of oral and written creativity.

The sources available for our investigation are spread over several categories. They include theoretical treatises (Aristotle, Cicero, Quintilian, Menander Rhetor, and others); oratory practice (including Isocrates, Latin panegyrics); testimonies about lost works, for example, Philostratus' *Lives of the Sophists* and references in the Byzantine encyclopedia entitled *Suda*; reflections on praise in a wide range of literary, historical, and philosophical works (Plato and Lucian, among others); inscriptions; and papyri. In addition to their chronological and geographical range, these sources are characterized by their diversity, as they comprise actual speeches as well as speculative and documentary texts. The history of epideictic rhetoric extends to both oratorical productions (and their relationship with society, usage, and institutions) and reflexive and conceptual elaboration, which took place in teaching, in theoreticians' research, and in philosophers' discussions. Any study must confront this methodological plurality in order to resituate the object within its own multiple territories—because every encomium is at once a literary work, a moral problem, and a social rite.

Our initial aim will be to establish rhetorical praise as a historical object, by defining it, by describing it in its context, and by retracing its evolution. This is the purpose of the first chapter, which marks out the stages of the development of the prose encomium, and of its crystallization as a rhetorical genre, from its first realizations in Classical Greece to the triumph of epideictic eloquence in the Greco-Roman world. This mutation meant the establishment of a new global rhetorical order in which public speaking was no longer limited to the tribunals and the assemblies, but also had a place in ceremonies. Repositioned in its historical context, this mutation reveals its political and social causes.

Chapter 2 analyzes the technique of praise, as stipulated by the theoreticians and used by the orators: the "commonplaces" (*topoi*) and their meaning, the different types of speeches, and the tropes and figures of style. The interest of this technique goes well beyond technical processes. It belongs to intellectual and cultural history, what French scholars called a "history of mentalities" (*histoire des mentalités*), as it reflects the wider mind-sets of educated groups for long durations of time.

The third chapter discusses the role of the technique and the tensions that praise can carry. It is necessary to assess the critiques leveled at encomia in antiquity, notably by the philosophers, in order to propose a global interpretation of this oratory form and explain the reasons for its success. Such balance can be achieved by examining the missions assigned to the epideictic orators, the function their words fulfilled, and the messages they delivered. Certain questions about the function of epideictic speeches must be posed in sociological terms. Epideictic rhetoric's chief function is a social one. It gives a shape to the representations and common beliefs of the group; it renders explicit, and justifies, accepted values; and on occasion it even offers lessons in new values.

The topic of epideictic rhetoric has yet to benefit from all the progress of current research on rhetoric. In the final chapter we indicate some paths for interpretation: what the speeches leave unspoken (hidden messages, idiosyncratic positions, veiled criticisms); a psychopathology of encomium (envy, flattery, disgust); religious epideictic (hymn, etc.); and comparative epideictic.

ACKNOWLEDGMENTS

This book originated in a seminar delivered by the author at the Rhetoric Society of America (RSA) meeting in May 2012 in Philadelphia and sponsored by the International Society for the History of Rhetoric (ISHR). I would like to remember Michael Leff (1941–2010), a great scholar of rhetoric who, in his capacity as a president of the RSA, first invited me to conduct this seminar. Mike and I knew each other for a long time. We both participated in the inaugural session of the ISHR in 1977 in Zurich, and we saw each other at several meetings over the years. I had the pleasure of welcoming Mike to Strasbourg in 2007, at the time of the sixteenth biennial meeting of the ISHR, where he gave a wonderful lecture, "The Expedient, the Honorable, and the Sacred: Rhetorical *Topoi* and the Religious Imperative." The text of that lecture has been published (Leff 2009), and it is probably one of the last articles Mike wrote that he could have seen in print before his death. The present book is dedicated to the memory of Michael Leff.

Mike and I discussed the subject of this seminar, and it was he, along with my dear friend in rhetoric, Larry Green, former president of the ISHR, who urged me to speak about epideictic rhetoric.

I warmly thank Larry Green, who organized the seminar, and Debra Hawhee, who played a decisive part in the publication of the book. I was fortunate to receive encouragement from these internationally known experts in the field of rhetoric, and I am in their debt for much help in revising what I have written.

My thanks are also due to Krista Ratcliffe, who succeeded Michael Leff as the head of the RSA; Kathie Cesa, RSA membership director; and Katherine Burton and Concetta Seminara, publishers at Taylor and Francis Group, which sponsored the seminar. All of these individuals contributed to the success of an experience that was memorable for me in many ways, above all for the hospitality and liveliness of the rhetorical community that welcomed me in Philadelphia, at the Loews Hotel, and in the historical reading room of the Athenaeum.

I recall the suggestive conversations on rhetoric I had with Marjorie Woods.

I am grateful to all the colleagues and researchers who participated in the seminar: in addition to the colleagues already mentioned above, Janet Atwill, Kathleen Bingham, Joshua Butcher, Brad Cook, Richard Graff, Katie Homar, Susan Jarratt, Robert King, Kathleen Lamp, Ilon Lauer, Arabella Lyon, Kerri Morris, Ellen Quandahl, James Selby, Vessela Valiavitcharska, Lisa Villadsen, and Susan Wells. Comments and discussions after my lectures were fruitful, and I deeply appreciated the patience and competence that my auditors brought to the argument.

Interesting exchanges of ideas took place with Susan Green, William FitzGerald, Ryan Stark, and Art Walzer.

William Higgins and Zoe Adams were of invaluable help to me in the preparation of the English text of the lectures.

I thank Jerry Murphy and Susan Jarratt for their insightful and generous comments.

The pages that follow retain the spirit of the original seminar. I have thoroughly revised and documented the text of the lectures and have added much, but I have sought neither to cover all aspects of the subject exhaustively nor to give information on every individual epideictic author. The aim is to offer a handy synthesis. This book has of course much in common with my 1993 French book on the same subject, even though my ideas have developed on some points. By comparison the present book goes less into details, while on the other hand it presents new trends and issues and tries to take into account recent publications and discoveries.

A NOTE ON SOURCES

For the reader's convenience, when citing ancient authors and texts, I am using the editions and translations found in the Loeb Classical Library, as available. For Isocrates, however, I am using Mirhady and Too's and Papillon's translations in the Oratory of Classical Greece series (Mirhady and Too 2000; Papillon 2004); for Aristotle's *Rhetoric*, I am using Kennedy's translation (Kennedy 1991). When there is no Loeb volume, other important sources are cited from the editions and/or translations listed here.

Aelius Aristides: Behr 1981–1986

Alexander, son of Numenius, *Fragment on Praise*: Spengel 1853–1856:3.1–6

Apuleius, *Florida*: Hilton, in Harrison 2001

Corpus Hermeticum: Copenhaver 1992

Gorgias, *Encomium of Helen*: MacDowell 1982

Greek Preliminary Exercises (*Progymnasmata*): Kennedy 2003

Gregory Thaumaturgus, *Address of Thanksgiving to Origen*: Slusser 1998

Himerius: Penella 2007

Latin panegyrics: Nixon and Rodgers 1994

Libanius (except the works found in Norman's Loeb volumes): Foerster and Richtsteig 1903–1927; Gibson 2008

Menander Rhetor: Russell and Wilson 1981

Pseudo–Aelius Aristides, *Rhetoric*: Patillon 2002

Pseudo–Dionysius of Halicarnassus, *Rhetoric*: Usener and Radermacher 1899–1929:6.253–387 (Greek text); Russell and Wilson 1981 (English translation of chaps. 1–7)

Suda (Suidas' Lexicon): Adler 1928–1938

EPIDEICTIC RHETORIC

ONE

THE UNSTOPPABLE RISE OF EPIDEICTIC

THE PRACTICE OF PRAISE IN CLASSICAL GREECE

The birth of rhetorical praise took place in Athens, after the Greco-Persian wars. Poetical praise had long existed (for example in Pindar's victory odes). Concerning prose, we first hear talk of eulogy speeches with the genre of the funeral oration (*epitaphios logos*), in the decade 470–461 BC.[1] Preserved specimens include Gorgias' fragment, Thucydides 2.35–46, Lysias' *Oration* 2, Demosthenes' *Oration* 60, and Hyperides' *Oration* 6.

From a rhetorical point of view, *epitaphioi logoi* are already a complex form of speech, as they combine the funeral eulogy, the essential element, with exhortation and with consolation, and even with lamentation; the eulogy itself is based on an equally complex object, which draws together the dead whose funeral is being celebrated, the fallen heroes from previous wars, and all the Athenians of the past and the present. The orator executed this program by following, albeit with some variations, a plan and employing commonplaces which appear to have been consecrated through usage very early on. The *epitaphios* was less a literary form than a civic institution, an integral part of the Epitaphia festival. It had an institutional function and translated a civic ideal.

In Athens there were also encomia written by the sophists and constituting literary compositions not intended for any institutional use, for example Gorgias' *Encomium of Helen*,[2] or paradoxical encomia (encomium of salt, cited by Isocrates, *Encomium of*

Helen 12, and Plato, *Symposium* 177b; encomia of cooking pots, pebbles, and mice by Polycrates[3]).

Isocrates finally introduced eulogy aiming at an individual object with the *Evagoras*, published around 365 BC. The preface (8) proclaims that this speech is the first eulogy in prose to a contemporary:

> I know that what I am about to do is difficult—praising a man's excellence through a speech. The greatest proof of this is that those who concern themselves with philosophy venture to speak on many other subjects of every different kind, but none of them has ever attempted to write on this matter. (Trans. Too [Mirhady and Too 2000:142])

The novelty of this speech was threefold: it was praising an individual (Evagoras, the king of Cypriot Salamis), as opposed to the collective character seen in the *epitaphios logos*, and a contemporary figure, as opposed to the mythological heroes seen in the paradoxical encomia, and it was written in prose. This innovation was soon adopted, for instance in the funerary eulogy of Gryllus, son of Xenophon, in 362 (Diogenes Laertius, *Lives of Eminent Philosophers* 2.55), or in the *Agesilaus* of Xenophon.

In practice, however, the use of epideictic remained rather limited in the Classical period (fifth and fourth centuries BC). It consisted mainly of civically sponsored funeral orations over soldiers fallen for their country (the *epitaphioi logoi*), as found in a small number of the works of sophists and orators, and of sophistic compositions. It was far less common and illustrious than the other two categories of oratory, judicial or forensic speeches and deliberative speeches. Demosthenes eclipsed Isocrates.

THE CREATION OF THE EPIDEICTIC GENUS

The practice of praise was accompanied by educational activity. Plato demonstrates in the *Phaedrus*, with the example of Lysias' speech, that the sophistic encomiastic compositions, read before disciples, took on the role of models (227cff.). Gorgias composed speeches of praise and blame for educational purposes and added theoretical indications to them (Aristotle, *Rhetoric* 3.1418a34–38). Isocrates was interested in the pedagogy of encomium.[4]

The first to isolate the notion of epideictic rhetoric was Aristotle, in the context of ordering the three genera of discourse. But the basis for Aristotle's classification had been laid out in various discussions, about praise and about *epideixis*.

Isocrates positions praise as an oratory form, by the side of other forms. The preface of the *Encomium of Helen* (14–15) distinguishes praise and apology. Elsewhere, Isocrates distinguishes praise (*enkōmion*) and advice (*sumboulē*) as two contrasting types of discourse (*Letters* 2.1, 9.1, 9.6). In a remarkable passage from *On the Peace* (27), written in 356 BC, he distinguishes accusation, praise, and advice:

> Someone who tries to address you on subjects that are out of the ordinary and wants to change your view must touch on many different matters and make his argument rather lengthy, recalling certain things, criticizing others, commending others, and giving advice on still others, for even with all this, it is only with difficulty that someone might lead you to a better understanding. (Trans. Papillon [2004:142])

The last three verbs in this list ("criticizing," "commending," "giving advice"; in Greek, *katēgoresai, epainesai, sumbouleusai*) announce the tripartition of the rhetorical genera, although these are as yet merely constituent elements, not autonomous types of discourse.

As for *epideixis*, the verb *epideiknunai*—particularly in middle voice, *epideiknusthai*—meant "to give an exhibition," "to show one's talent," in whichever domain; for an orator, *epideixis* signified a "lecture." For instance, the Hippocratic treatises *On Winds* and *On Art* constitute two medical *epideixeis*, in an ornate style.[5] The *epideixis* was above all the specialty of the sophists, notably well known from the numerous allusions in Plato; Plato even coined the expression "art of *epideixis*" (*epideiktikē [tekhnē]*), "a ri-

TABLE I

	Constituent Elements					
Rhetorical Genera	*Role of the Audience*	*Content*	*Tense Concerned*	*End* (*Telos*)	*Most Appropriate Argument Type*	*Style*
Deliberative genus	Judge	Exhortation	Future	Useful	Example	Agonistic
		Dissuasion		Harmful		
Judicial genus	Judge	Accusation	Past	Just	Enthymeme	Agonistic
		Defense		Unjust		
Epideictic genus	Spectator	Praise	Principally the present	Beautiful	Amplification	Written
		Blame		Ugly		

diculous name," which he used when defining the art of sophistic (*Sophist* 224b):

> Stranger: Then will you give the same name [i.e., *merchant*] to him who buys up knowledge and goes about from city to city exchanging his wares for money?
> Theaetetus: Certainly.
> Stranger: One part of this soul-merchandising might very properly be called the art of display [*epideiktikē*], might it not? But since the other part, though no less ridiculous than the first, is nevertheless a traffic in knowledge, must we not call it by some name akin to its business?
> Theaetetus: Certainly. (Trans. Fowler [1921:293])

The *epideixis* was given at the occasion of a festival, at Olympia for example, or it could also be saved for a more limited audience. Its content was variable: it could be a mythical tale (the myth of Protagoras in the *Protagoras* of Plato; Xenophon's apologue of Prodicus, about Heracles) or an encomium (Isocrates' *Encomium of Helen*)[6]. Praise was but one possible content of the *epideixis*. In any case, the *epideixis* was an exhibition with no practical finality, unlike speeches which discussed real interests and led people to take action. *Epideixis* contrasted with true advocacy and with political deliberation.

The Aristotelian system was constructed on this basis. Aristotle's *Rhetoric* is the first treatise that defines epideictic in a technical way. Aristotle makes epideictic one of the three rhetorical genera, defining it as the category that comprises speeches of praise and blame, in the context of ordering the three genera of discourse, which can be summarized in the form of a table (*Rhetoric* 1.1358a36–1359a5, 1368a26–33; 3.1414a8–19): see the facing page.

With these definitions, praise enters right into the field of rhetoric. Aristotle joined praise and *epideixis* together, in order to create a new concept: encomium. Validating the development of praise in oratorical practice and in education, Aristotle gave it a name, a space, an aim: praise (and blame, its opposite) occupied a full third of the material on oratory.[7]

In the same period (second half of the fourth century BC), the treatise usually called *Rhetoric to Alexander* presented a system that, while not identical to Aristotle's, is pretty close to it and also isolates as a separate category speeches of praise and blame. This treatise is falsely attributed to Aristotle, and modern philologists consider it to have been written by either Anaximenes of Lampsacus or an anonymous writer. The author of this work initially distinguishes three genera of discourse (demegoric, epideictic, judiciary), which are then divided into seven "species" (*eidē*): "suasion and dissuasion" (*protreptikon* and *apotreptikon*), "praise and blame" (*enkōmiastikon* and *psektikon*), "accusation and defense" (*katēgorikon* and *apologikon*), and "examination" (*exetastikon*) (1.1). This text can therefore be seen to offer the same doctrine as Aristotle's *Rhetoric*, with three genera, each of which is subdivided in two; the "examination" fits within this schema, because it has very little autonomous existence and is more often found mixed with the other species (*Rhetoric to Alexander* 37.1).

Certain editors have suggested that the text we read in the manuscripts is the result of a remaking, an ancient forgery, that was intended to bring the treatise in line with Aristotelian doctrine; but this seems unlikely. Whatever the reason, the epideictic genus is present de facto in the *Rhetoric to Alexander.*

As this treatise appears contemporary to Aristotle's *Rhetoric*, the question engaging scholars is whether one influenced the other particularly, since the two texts demonstrate numerous convergences. A range of hypotheses has been advanced, from that of a direct influence to that of a common source, and it seems difficult to choose between them. Whichever it may be, Aristotle's is the one that best illuminates the notion of the epideictic genre, while the *Rhetoric to Alexander* stands as proof that Aristotle was not isolated and that epideictic was discussed elsewhere at the end of the Classical period.

PROBLEMS OF DEFINITION AND TERMINOLOGY

Hereafter begins a long history of the notion of the "epideictic genus." Theophrastus, Aristotle's disciple and successor, circulated and extended his master's thoughts, notably in respect to rhetorical praise.[8] The doctrine of Aristotle's *Rhetoric*—if not always the text—was largely known by the rhetoricians and profoundly influenced them. There is a continued meditation on the classification of the genera and particularly on the epideictic genus in ancient rhetoric.[9]

The Greek and Latin rhetoricians—for example Hermagoras, Cicero, Quintilian, and the authors of *progymnasmata*—almost universally adopted the division of the three rhetorical genera. In Cicero, *On the Orator* (1.137, 141) Crassus says:

> I will not deny that I learned those commonplace and well-worn maxims of teachers in general. . . . Again I heard that, of such questions as are distinct from general issues, some have their place in courts of justice, others in deliberations; while there was yet a third kind, which had to do with the extolling or reviling of particular persons. (Trans. Sutton and Rackham [1942:97, 99])

This general acceptance of the Aristotelian system is not without some minor queries, for instance about the word most suited to referring to the "genera" of discourse. Aristotle employs *genos*; but others preferred to employ *eidos* "species" (Aristotle himself once used this word), or even *meros* "part." This question of titling was abundantly disputed, as Quintilian shows (*The Orator's Education* 3.3.14–15).

The Aristotelian structure is further shaken by discussion regarding the sufficiency of the tripartition. Considering that the list of three genera did not convey the full diversity of the oratory forms, certain rhetoricians tried to complete it by creating supplementary genera. As such, we find history,[10] or individual discussions and dialogues, as opposed to public speeches.[11] Others went much further still in the multiplication of the genera, bringing them to a total of as many as thirty: this extreme position is discussed particularly by Cicero (*On the Orator* 2.43–64) and Quintilian. Here are the words of Quintilian (*The Orator's Education* 3.4.1, 3):

> Whether there are three or more of these is disputed. . . . Indeed, if we place the function of praise and blame in the third part, on what "kind" are we to think ourselves engaged when we complain, console, pacify, excite, frighten, encourage, instruct, explain obscurities, narrate, plead for mercy, give thanks, congratulate, reproach, abuse, describe, command, renounce, wish, opine, and so on and so forth? (Trans. Russell [2001:2.31])

These discussions reveal a certain dissatisfaction with the Aristotelian schema. Many rhetoricians saw that the three genera only sketched out the broadest lines of the field of rhetoric. The orator's task is not reduced to counseling, defending, praising (and their opposites): these terms represent perhaps the principal tendency of the majority of ancient rhetorical speeches, but eloquence also fulfilled other functions.[12]

THE HELLENISTIC GREEK WORLD AND THE ROMAN REPUBLIC

In the Greek Hellenistic period, which extends from Alexander's death to the beginning of Augustus' principate, the evidence for epideictic is poor. This period is less well known than the others in terms of the history of rhetoric. No treatises or speeches are preserved. It is necessary to search in the inscriptions, papyri, and fragments to find traces. Epideictic rhetoric was of continued interest to the theoreticians and the orators of this period, although our information is incomplete. The most interesting examples include a papyrus which contains the remnants, albeit badly mutilated, of five encomia in honor of mythological heroes, certainly as school compositions,[13] and an encomium of the goddess Isis on an engraved stone at Maroneia in Thrace.[14]

In Rome, the first epideictic speeches were, as in Athens, funeral orations (*laudationes funebres*).[15] Contrary to the democratic and collective character of the Athenian funeral oration, those in Rome were speeches in the honor of members of the main families, which praised the deceased and their *gens*. Funeral oration aside, traditional Roman eloquence ignored praise discourse: Cicero does not cite a single one in *Brutus*. Praise had an additional role in the tribunal, with the old custom of *laudatio iudicialis* (Suetonius, *The Lives of the Caesars*: *Augustus* 56): after the pleas, the accused was allowed to produce *laudatores*, distinct from the defense witnesses, who painted him in the most favorable light possible.

Roman treatises reflect this additive role of praise. The *Rhetoric to Herennius* and Cicero's treatises mention the epideictic genre, but consider it secondary to the deliberative genre, and above all to the judicial genre. Rhetorical praise does not belong to the national tradition, Antonius says in Cicero's *On the Orator* 2.341:

> We Romans do not much practise the custom of panegyrics. . . . Our Roman commendatory speeches that we make in the forum have either the bare and unadorned brevity of evidence to a person's character or are written to be delivered as a funeral speech, which is by no means a suitable occasion for parading one's distinction in rhetoric. (Trans. Sutton and Rackham [1942:457])

Toward the end of his life, Cicero became more interested in praise.[16] In *Divisions of Oratory* (69–70) he highlighted the moral functions of praise and of blame, and he inserted morsels of praise in certain of his speeches. The *Second Verrine Oration* contains an encomium of Sicily and a description of Syracuse (2.2–9; 4.117–119; passages cited in Cicero, *Orator* 210). The speech in favor of Manilius' law (*Pro lege Manilia* 27–49) offers a good and proper praise to Pompey. But these innovations were still limited.

EPIDEICTIC RHETORIC IN THE GREEK WORLD IN THE IMPERIAL PERIOD

A veritable triumph of epideictic rhetoric marked the Imperial period. Throughout the five centuries of the Roman Empire, from the Augustan settlement in 27 BC to the death of Romulus Augustulus in AD 476, very large numbers of epideictic speeches were delivered, in Latin and Greek, in pagan as well as Christian contexts. The epideictic genus, which started as rhetoric's poor relation, became under the Roman Empire its most esteemed and prominent. The following pages concentrate mainly on the first three centuries of the period.

Epideictic rhetoric blossomed in the Greek world within the milieu of the Second Sophistic. The sophists of the Second Sophistic formed a professional, social, and cultural network. Teaching rhetoric, public speaking, political influence, fame, wealth, and globe-trotting typified their lives. Professors and lecturers, they were connected to the Roman government and the civic aristocracies. Despite its geographical extension, the sophistic milieu was culturally isomorphic. The Second Sophistic benefited from the coherence of the Greco-Roman world during this period. This coherence was increased by the personal relationships which often united the sophists. They knew each other, directly or through mutual contact, listened to each other, and read each other's work. The Second Sophistic, a formerly disparaged movement, has earned its place in the domain of classical studies, and more and more studies have been dedicated to the subject, particularly during the last three or four decades. Gradually, the Second Sophistic is becoming more known and more recognized.[17]

This examination of Greek epideictic rhetoric in the Imperial period will take into account three interrelated domains of activity: teaching, theoretical research, and oratorical practice.

From the Imperial age onward, the encomium was included in the standard cycle of rhetoric's "preliminary exercises" (*progymnasmata*). Praise was a school topic, and scholastic encomia, sporadically attested in earlier periods, became conventional in the syllabus. The main authors on those subjects are Aelius Theon, Hermogenes (or Pseudo-Hermogenes), Aphthonius, and Nicolaus.[18] Since rhetoric was the "core" of the ancient curriculum, we may conclude that anyone who received a quality education (that is, elite, powerful males) was trained in the rhetoric of the encomium. Some papyri bear witness to the scholastic practice of praise.[19] True, the curriculum for a rhetoric student consisted of various preliminary exercises and of declamation (which did not include praise, as it was either judicial or deliberative): encomium (*enkōmion*) was only one of the preliminary exercises. But a further, more in-depth teaching of epideictic eloquence took place through school contests and academic ceremonies.

Young people and adolescents took part in competitions in the school setting. Attic inscriptions give us an indication of the program of festivals that punctuated the ephebic calendar in Athens: in the second century AD these festivals included literary competitions comprising a praise trial (*enkōmion*).[20] In all probability these praises were addressed, in prose or in verse, to the entity to whom each festival was dedicated—god, hero, emperor, or member of the Imperial family. The ephebes certainly had a rhetoric teacher who taught them how to compose and pronounce their encomia. They were also taught other oratory forms, but only encomium was used in competitions, which demonstrates its importance in the society of the period.

Academic life also included ceremonies during which epideictic speeches were made. For example, according to Menander Rhetor II (430–434, 396–399, 391, 392), a student leaving his hometown to complete his studies in a large university city would give a farewell speech to his fellow citizens, certainly in the presence of the teachers and students from the local school. When, having finished his education, he left the large university city, he gave another farewell speech, to which either a fellow student or a teacher would reply with a bidding of safe return. Once returned to his hometown, the student must again give a talk, to express his joy at having returned. This means that a total of four epideictic speeches were made over the course of one university departure. In schools of rhetoric, the students first defended their oratory skills under the critical eye of their master. The teaching of epideictic rhetoric thus appears more targeted than one would have initially thought. The study of theoretical treatises leads to a similar observation.

Rhetorical theory in the Imperial period appears to have been principally devoted to deliberative and judicial discourses (either real or fictional, that is, declamatory, speeches). The epideictic genus is nonetheless discussed in Quintilian's *The Orator's Educa-*

tion (3.7) and in a passage of the *Rhetoric* falsely attributed to Aelius Aristides (1.160–166). Above all, and for the first time in the history of rhetoric, the Imperial period saw the appearance of treatises devoted exclusively to encomium. These works fall into two groups. The first of these is represented by the extract attributed to Alexander, son of Numenius (second century AD), and by the *Division of Epideictic Speeches* (*Diairesis tōn epideiktikōn*) by Menander Rhetor I (third century AD), which is unfortunately incomplete.[21] It is based on the division of subjects of praise; that is to say, the treatise successively takes up the praise of gods, of cities, of men, of animals, and of inanimate things. Menander explains this division in the following way (*Division of Epideictic Speeches* 331–332):

> Epideictic speeches, then, fall under the two headings of blame and praise. . . . The division of "blame" has no subdivision. "Praise" of some kind, on the other hand, occurs sometimes in relation to gods, sometimes in relation to mortal objects. When it relates to gods, we speak of "hymns," and we divide these in turn according to the god concerned. . . . Praise of mortal objects comprises (i) praise of cities and countries, (ii) praise of living creatures. The heading of cities and countries is not divisible further. . . . Praise of living creatures deals either with the rational (man) or with the non-rational. Let us pass over praise of "man." The non-rational then includes (a) land animals, (b) water-animals. Again, we set aside the subject of water-animals; the other category, land-animals, falls into two classes, the flying and the walking. At the conclusion of all this, we shall proceed from the animate to the inanimate. (Trans. Russell and Wilson [1981:3–5])

The second group is represented by two third-century works, the first seven chapters of the *Rhetoric* by Pseudo–Dionysius of Halicarnassus and the treatise *On Epideictic Speeches* (*Peri epideiktikōn*) by Menander Rhetor II. These treatises classify the epideictic material according to types of speech: praise to the emperor, arrival speech, farewell speech, epithalamium, funeral oration, address to a governor, panegyric, etc. It is imperative not to underestimate the importance of this second group, which has no equivalent in the treatises dedicated to the two other genera: encomium is no longer to be seen as an abstract rhetorical form, but is rather a social practice, embodied in concrete speech circumstances. These treatises represent only the known part of the theoretical discussion, which was more abundant, but the majority of which has been lost.

Examination of the extant treatises and of the *testimonia* on lost treatises justifies the conclusion that epideictic theory, after the silence of the Hellenistic period, enjoyed renewal and growth under the Roman Empire, maintaining a constant dialogue with the development of oratorical practice. The close connection these treatises have with practical oratory is absolutely clear: they envision actual speeches, on contemporary topics, and theorize within the context of the living spoken word. This radically distinguishes epideictic theory from deliberative and judicial treatises of the Imperial period, which deal primarily with declamation.

As for oratorical practice, judicial and deliberative oratory did play a role in the Imperial period. Judicial oratory evidently was used before the empire's tribunals. There was also deliberative oratory, at the level of municipal politics, undertaken in front of the council and assembly of the cities, and at the level of provincial assemblies. The cities had some room to maneuver under Roman authority. The corpus of Dio Chrysostom, for example, includes a series of speeches which clearly illustrate the realities of municipal politics (*Orations* 38–51). Embassy rhetoric flourished. Major political oratory, however—in the traditional sense of vital questions, such as wars, alliances, taxes, etc., debated before a sovereign people—no longer existed, because of the Imperial regime. Such changes in the political climate help to account for the development of epideictic.

Indeed, epideictic oratory saw an unprecedented development in the Greek world of the Imperial period, and our sources are much richer than in preceding periods. Within this abundant documentation it is necessary to distinguish already attested epideictic forms, which developed over the course of the Imperial period, from actual innovations. The development of already existing forms is represented by encomia of persons and praise of cities and gods. Orators praised emperors, provincial governors, magistrates, and notable city figures. They also praised women: the empress, or the emperor's mistress, for instance. They praised cities and monuments. Examples of encomia of emperors and cities are studied later in this chapter. As for gods, the rules of prose hymns, a notable conquest with respect to the rich tradition of poetic hymns, are outlined in the treatises of Quintilian, of Alexander, son of Numenius, and of Menander Rhetor I; in practice, Aelius Aristides offers a rich collection of rhetorical hymns to various gods.[22]

Praise competitions are an interesting case. The second and third centuries were a time of intense activity for Greek contests. The first-rank, pan-Hellenic, and sacred contests, whose number had already increased over the Hellenic period, multiplied at the instigation of the emperors, particularly Hadrian; local contests prospered, and Italy entered into the "circuit" of Greek competitions. The contests consisted of two parts, the "gymnic," or sport-oriented, trials, and the "musical" trials, which were devoted to the arts of the Muses and literary endeavors.[23] Inscriptions reveal the regular presence of prose encomia in the "musical" contests.

The first category of sources is composed of the inscriptions that give the list of the trials for a given contest. For example, in Corinth, the contest called "Kaisareia" included encomium trials in prose and in verse in honor of emperors and members of the Imperial family, namely Augustus, Tiberius, and Livia.[24] At Oenoanda, in what is now southwestern Turkey, the Dēmostheneia included encomium trials in prose and in verse in honor of the founder of the contest.[25] To this category belongs an important discovery made in 2004 in Naples on the occasion of the building of a metro line. Among various remnants of monuments a portico was found, the wall of which was covered with engraved marble slabs. Examination of the nearly one thousand preserved fragments revealed an inscription dating from Domitian's reign (last quarter of first century AD). This long text gives the list of the winners of numerous editions of the important contest called "Italika Rhōmaia Sebasta Isolympia." This contest comprised several encomium trials, in verse and in prose, in honor of emperors and members of the Imperial family.[26]

The second category of sources comprises the inscriptions that honor an author of encomia (*enkōmiastēs*) who won in one or many competitions.[27] There were also bilingual competitions, in Greek and Latin, for example at the Capitolia in Rome: when Domitian instituted this competition in AD 86, it included two eloquence trials, one Greek and the other Latin, which had the theme of praise of Jupiter Capitolinus (Quintilian, *The Orator's Education* 3.7.4; Suetonius, *The Lives of the Caesars*: *Domitian* 4). The sources also cite the example of a Greek and Latin eloquence competition opened by Caligula at Lyon: it seems that the defeated competitors had to erase their writing with a sponge or with their tongue, and that some of them were made to—in an even crueler punishment—compose the winner's encomium (Suetonius, *The Lives of the Caesars*: *Caligula* 20).

Praise had to take a place in the Greek competitions when it became obligatory to praise Roman personages, particularly the emperors. It must be noted that encomium was still not the most enjoyed trial. For the contests providing payment in cash, the prize lists reveal that the encomium trials in verse and in prose were among the least valued, while the comedians and tragedians were allotted the highest prizes.[28] After the trumpet and the herald, which signaled a sort of lifting of the curtain, the encomiasts in prose and in verse played a role akin to today's performance hosts, paying homage to the tutelary powers of the competition, before introducing the musicians and the dramatic artists, who were preferred. When the competition was both musical and gymnastic, the athletic trials were even more profoundly appreciated than the literary and artistic trials.

The epideictic innovations of the Imperial period mainly consist in the proliferation of the kinds of occasional discourses. Throughout the empire, the circumstances of public and private life were punctuated by ceremonial allocutions. An important point here is the rapport of epideictic rhetoric with poetry. For numerous sorts of discourse in prose, there were precedents in poetry.[29] The move from poetic to prose forms is a crucial part of epideictic's historical development, and the contribution of rhetoric during the Imperial period was one of employing oratorical prose to punctuate the circumstances of public and private life. Rhetoric isolated different epideictic forms and equipped them with a content that was inspired by social practice, poetic models, and the previous rhetorical tradition of praise. The story is one of re-ordering, an annexing and a codification responding to the necessities of the circumstances. But of course verse never disappeared, remaining in use to express praise throughout ancient times. The history of encomiastic poetry is a parallel and rival topic compared with epideictic rhetoric, although it is only possible to touch upon it here.[30]

For the most part the circumstances inviting epideictic rhetoric fall into two large categories, journeys and family events. Under the title of "journeys," a sample case is that of the speech intended to welcome a sovereign or a governor. The function of celebrating royal "entries" is very old. Already in Aeschylus, Agamemnon is welcomed by a speech by the chorus leader when he arrives in Argos (*Agamemnon* 782ff.). During the Imperial period, the "entry" (Lat. *adventus*; Gk. *apantēsis*) ceremony was very frequent; a solemn cortege gathered to meet the emperor or governor arriving in the city.[31] The event could be marked with a poem, but more often rhetorical speeches were employed. There are two instances of this type of discourse from Aelius Aristides (*Orations* 17 and 21). In the third century, Callinicus gave a speech welcoming Gallienus (this speech is lost; its existence is known through the Byzantine encyclopedia *Suda* K 231); and in the fourth, Libanius gave a similar speech for Julian (*Orations* 13).

At the same time, the theoreticians were laying down rules for this oratorical form. The *prosphōnēmatikos* (address) of Pseudo–Dionysius of Halicarnassus (5.272–277) corresponds to the first form of Menander Rhetor II's *epibatērios* ("discourse of arrival," that is to say, marking the arrival of the governor; 378–382). Menander Rhetor II (414–418) also defined the *prosphōnētikos*, a simple encomium of a governor, which was notably used for his arrival. Apparently the *epibatērios* was given outside the city, when the population went to meet the person arriving; the *prosphōnēmatikos* was given within the walls, once the person arriving had been escorted to the city and made his entrance there. The most frequent use of this type of speech was to welcome the arrival of the Roman governors to the provinces and to signal their movements within them.

The "invitation speech" (*klētikos*) had a wide usage. It could be addressed to a governor, to invite him to visit a city or to honor a festival with his presence, but also to a god, to solicit his coming (Menander Rhetor I, 334–336; Menander Rhetor II, 424–430). One extant example of this is a Latin panegyric (7) which begs Constantine to visit Autun, the orator's homeland.

The arrival speech is made by the traveler who arrives. In Menander Rhetor II's work (382–387), this is the second form of *epibatērios* ("arriver's speech," given by the person being welcomed). Lucian's work includes many speeches of this type: *My Native Land*, upon his return to his homeland; *Amber; or, The Swans, Herodotus; or, Aetion, Harmonides*, and *The Scythian; or, The Consul*, upon arrival before a foreign audience.

In addition to the speech by the person arriving, there was the farewell speech. Here also there were poetic precedents, such as the farewells of Odysseus to the Phaeacians or the *ultima verba* so often appearing in tragedies.[32] In rhetoric, the eloquence of a departure speech was taught at school, since the curriculum would suggest ethologic subjects of *prosopopoeia* or *ethopoeia* (both terms meaning "imitation of the character of a person supposed to be speaking"), such as "What words would a man say to his wife when leaving on a journey?" or "What words would Achilles say to Deidamia when about to go to war?"[33] Menander Rhetor II (393–394, 430–434) calls this "farewell speech" (*suntaktikos logos* or *suntaktikē lalia*). Attested examples include Gregory Thaumaturgus' speech when leaving Caesarea, where he had been taught by Origen (third century AD), or *Oration* 11 of Himerius and *Oration* 42 of Gregory of Nazianzus (fourth century AD).

Those who remain express wishes for safe onward journeys (*propemptikos*, "valediction"). Here again the poetic tradition is ancient and abundant. But this form of discourse appears as a rhetorical genre only in the Imperial period. Once again the Imperial period marks the beginning of a prose treatment of subjects that were previously written in verse. Rhetoric has taken over from poetry. A good example is the ninth piece of Apuleius' *Florida*. Menander Rhetor II (395–399) theorizes on this type of speech by highlighting the variety of its uses, as it can just as well be used when addressing a pupil, a fellow student, or a governor. The genre is well attested in Himerius (*Orations* 10, 12, 15, 31, 36).

After journeys, family events constitute the second large category of occasional speeches. Depending on the social position of the person praised (the *laudandus*), the speech would remain private or, alternatively, take on a more official character.

Funeral oration continued to develop and change as a genre. The collective form (*epitaphios*) mentioned at the beginning of this chapter no longer existed, so it seems, except in declamation form, insofar as it was linked to Athenian democracy,[34] but individual homage increased. Funeral orations were used not only for sovereigns but for private people.[35] Rhetorical consolations and laments grew in number, either as autonomous speeches or as parts of funeral orations.[36]

Addresses at weddings had taken place since the beginnings of Greek literature, in poetry, in the form of the marriage song and epithalamium. In line with the pattern seen elsewhere, it was during the Imperial period that the rhetoricians began to intervene in nuptial ceremonies.[37] In the second century, Pollux of Naucratis celebrated the marriage of Caesar Commodus with Crispina with an *epithalamios* (*Suda* Π 1951). The theoreticians discussed the subject. For instance, the *Rhetoric* of Pseudo-Dionysius of Halicarnassus (chaps. 2 and 4) distinguishes the "marriage speech" (*gamēlios* or *gamikos*), doubtless made on the occasion of the sacrifice to the gods of marriage (*gamēlioi theoi*), during the banquet at the home of the girl's father, and the "epithalamium," which took place after the conclusion of the marriage, that is to say in the groom's home and before the couple entered the nuptial chamber. In the fourth century we know of epithalamiums by Himerius (*Orations* 9 and 37) and by Choricius (*Orations* 5 and 6). It is important to specify that school rhetoric also addressed the subject of marriage in the form of the discussion concerning "whether one should marry" (e.g., Aelius Theon, *Exercises* 11[12].120).

The birthday speech also became part of a ceremony, in which were celebrated the anniversary of the birth of a deceased or living person, including sovereigns, the founders of philosophical schools, and private individuals; to these we must add the anniversaries of gods and of cities. During the Imperial period, the birthday of the reigning prince was celebrated, in Rome and in the provinces, with games and solemn *vota*. In private houses, the birthday of a family member might be the occasion of a banquet, accompanied by prayers or sacrifices to the "gods of birth" (*genethlioi theoi*). In such circumstances one would send letters and presents and compose poetry.[38] The poet Statius celebrated the anniversary of the birth of the deceased poet Lucan (*Silvae* 2.7).

Epideictic oratory made its entry onto this particular scene, not surprisingly, in the Imperial period. Pseudo-Dionysius of Halicarnassus (chap. 3) and Menander Rhetor II (412–413) laid out the rules of the birthday speech (*genethliakos*). The sophist Zenobius was the author of a *genethliakos* in honor of Hadrian Caesar (*Suda* Z 73). Aelius Aristides composed a speech for the birthday of his noble pupil, the young Apellas (*Oration* 30). However, it looks as if epideictic rhetoric had not provided for the celebration of the actual birth of a child, although this type of composition, distinct from the birthday encomium, had the freedom of the city in poetry (Callimachus, fr. 202 Pfeiffer; Statius, *Silvae* 4.7–8) and had earned its nobility thanks to Virgil's fourth *Eclogue*.

To judge the development of epideictic in the Imperial age precisely, two indicators may serve: the increased variety and the increased quantity of orations. Both lead to the same conclusion, and studying them will permit us to take epideictic rhetoric's true measure. First, let's consider the variety of orations. In Greek rhetoric of the Classical period—Aristotle, for example—and in Republican Latin rhetoric—Cicero—epideictic was thought of as a "pure" speech of praise, an encomium devoted to a single subject (usually a human being) and whose structure adhered to an internal logic, to some extent independent of the circumstances of the encomium's actual delivery. In contrast, epideictic under the Roman Empire is quite cognizant of the circumstances of the oration's delivery, especially the time, the place, the audience, and the purpose of the ceremony surrounding it. Thus considered, the oration is not an encomium pure and simple, suitable for all occasions, something generalized and abstract, but an oration specifically tailored to the requirements of the topic. Accordingly, epideictic rhetoric is no longer a monolithic genus; from this point on, it breaks down into various species.

This new approach was conceptually recognized and theorized under the Roman Empire. The encomium was thought of no longer as an abstract rhetorical form but rather as a social practice embodied in speeches undertaken for specific occasions. This diversification of speeches was accompanied by the development of a rich vocabulary in Greek and Latin. Each type of oration was given a technical name, many of which have been mentioned above: e.g., *epibatērios* (discourse of arrival; arriver's speech), *gamēlios* (marriage speech), *genethliakos* (birthday speech), *klētikos* (invitation speech), *propemptikos* (valediction), *prosphōnēmatikos* (address), and *suntaktikos* (farewell speech).

Such diversification went along with an increase in the quantity of speeches, the second indicator of transformation in the epideictic genre. Just think of the establishment of schools of rhetoric in all the cities of the Roman Empire; just imagine the birthdays, weddings, and funerals of leading citizens, the inaugurations, the banquets, the journeys, the festivals and contests, the movements of governors in the provinces and the influx of diplomatic missions to Rome, the homage rendered to every reigning emperor and to his deceased and deified predecessors. Add up the possible or obligatory orations in all these cases, and the potential corpus of epideictic rhetoric in the Imperial age, covering half a millennium and the entire extent of the Roman Empire, certainly comprises some hundreds of thousands of speeches. School lecture halls, patrician homes, theaters, and palaces buzzed with encomia, whether poorly recited or magnificently declaimed. The few dozen orations we still possess today can be understood only in relation to this immense and vanished corpus. They are the fragments of a frieze, the telltale signs of a social activity and a cultural shift.

EPIDEICTIC RHETORIC AND ROMAN CULTURE

Quintilian's *The Orator's Education* is testimony to the development of epideictic rhetoric in Rome during the period of the empire. Quintilian devotes a chapter to the epideictic genus (3.7), and this chapter contains some interesting elements. In addition to the encomium of men, which Quintilian's Roman predecessors already knew, the list of subjects is stretched to gods, cities, and even to monuments, places, and all sorts of things (3.7.6):

> The material is of course mainly to do with gods and men, but it can also be other animals and even inanimate objects. (Trans. Russell [2001:2.105])

Additionally, Quintilian no longer considers encomium to be a Greek genre; he highlights that the "Roman custom" (*mos Romanus*) permits it, in the form of "funeral laudations" (*funebres laudationes*), praise and blame inserted into advocacies or speeches in the Senate, and finally praises of Jupiter at the Capitoline competition (3.7.2–3):

> Roman custom, on the other hand, has found a place for this function [*sc.* praise and blame] in practical business. Funeral laudations are frequently attached to some public office and are often entrusted to magistrates by order of the Senate; to praise or discredit a witness is important in court; it is a permitted practice to let defendants have people to praise their character; and finally, the published speeches against Cicero's fellow candidates, against Lucius Piso, and against Clodius and Curio, contain invective, and yet were spoken as formal voting statements in the Senate. I do not deny that some themes of this kind are composed solely for display, for example panegyrics of the gods and great men of past ages, . . . the praise of Jupiter Capitolinus, the invariable theme of the sacred contest. (Trans. Russell [2001:2.103])

Quintilian can therefore be seen to recognize the existence of a Roman epideictic oratory (which Cicero had glimpsed and started to practice at the end of his life). The traditional forms, *laudatio funebris* and *laudatio iudicialis*, retain an essential role in his eyes; but he notes that agonistic encomium has just been made customary by Domitian, and that no subject is now out of the reach of Roman orators, at least in theory.

Oratorical practice, however, does not correspond fully to Quintilian's indications, as most of the preserved Latin epideictic orations are directed to men. To some extent this may be the result of the hazards in transmission of texts, but one gets the impression that Roman practice remained marked by the weight of national tradition. The encomium appeared in Roman preliminary exercises (Quintilian 2.1.11; 2.4.20). The masters discussed not only Greek subjects but also subjects drawn from national history. Quintilian (3.7.5, 18, 20–21) envisages the praises of Romulus, Numa, and Publicola, and the blame of Maelius, of M. Manlius, or of the Gracchi, either as exercises or in real speeches.

Next, the orators dedicated themselves to the *laudatio funebris*, which, private or public, was still practiced frequently under the principate. Examples of private funeral orations include engraved eulogies of Turia and Murdia, under Augustus (Dessau, *Inscriptiones Latinae Selectae* 8393–8394); compositions by Pliny the Younger on the son of his friend Spurinna (Pliny the Younger, *Letters* 3.10, 4.7); and the *Agricola* of Tacitus. Public funeral orations include the speech Tacitus, then consul, gave in honor of Verginius Rufus (Pliny, *Letters* 2.1.6); and eulogies to the emperors and the members of the imperial family.

A frequent oratory form was the *gratiarum actio* of the consuls. On the day of taking charge, the consuls had to give a speech to the Senate wherein they thanked the emperor who selected them. Preserved examples are the *Panegyricus to Trajan* by Pliny the Younger[39] and the thanks of Mamertinus to Julian (*Latin Panegyrics* 11). These works are important because they illustrate an often unrecognized epideictic form, that of the speech of thanks. Rhetorical theory does not define the speech of thanks. Even Pseudo–Dionysius of Halicarnassus and Menander Rhetor II ignore it, indicating that the theoreticians had a particular discomfort in allowing thanks into one of the three Aristotelian genera.

The Latin panegyrics show us even more circumstances in which the emperor was praised at the end of the third and during the fourth centuries (see p. 25). Faced with this predominance of encomia of men, and above all the emperor, we must assume that the other forms of praise were much less richly represented among the Romans than the Greeks.

Two characters played an important role in developing epideictic literature in Rome. Marcus Cornelius Fronto notably practiced paradoxical praise.[40] Apuleius wrote encomia of Carthage (*Florida* 18.36; 20) and hymns in prose: the hymn to Isis inserted into the *Metamorphoses* (11.25), and a lost speech about Aesculapius (*Apologia* 55; *Florida* 18.38). But Roman epideictic eloquence was by and large in retreat compared to that of the Greek-speaking provinces: the triumph of the encomium during the Imperial period mainly remains a Greek phenomenon.

A GLANCE AT LATE ANTIQUITY

Epideictic rhetoric resisted the crisis of the third century, as the treatises of Pseudo–Dionysius of Halicarnassus and of Menander Rhetor, which date back to this period, show, and as do the speeches (lost today, but attested in multiple sources) of the sophist Callinicus of Petra.[41] Even in periods of political crisis, the educational system was resistant to the difficulties of the hour, and ceremonies continued to be celebrated.

Epideictic rhetoric took on a new lustre in the period of Constantine, with Eusebius and the first Latin panegyrics. It developed further still during the fourth century, with Julian, Himerius, Themistius, Libanius, with their less famous colleagues, and with the Church Fathers.[42]

TWO EXAMPLES OF EPIDEICTIC RHETORIC'S HISTORICAL DEVELOPMENT

To complement this historical sketch, two examples illustrate the path of epideictic from its creation in Greece until the time of the

Roman Empire: the encomium of emperors and the encomium of cities.

As mentioned earlier, Isocrates was the first to add a political dimension to the rhetorical praise of an individual, in his eulogy of Evagoras. A few years later, Xenophon, in turn, eulogized the Spartan king Agesilaus, and thus begins the history of a particularly important subgenre of epideictic, the encomium of a sovereign.[43] After Isocrates and Xenophon, we hear in the sources of encomia of Alexander the Great (by Theopompus and Lamachus of Smyrna) and of Mithridates (by two Greeks resident at his court, Metrodorus of Skepsis and Aesop).[44] An orator named Potamo of Mytilene pulled off the tour de force of writing an encomium of Brutus and an encomium of Caesar.[45]

There are few royal encomia attested for the Hellenistic period. Other means of paying homage were apparently preferred during this time, from the awarding of an honorific title to the institution of a cult, accompanied by encomia in verse. In celebrating rulers, the rhetorical encomium encountered strong competition, and it was far from always having the upper hand. In the Roman Republic, there was no royal encomium, and with reason, but only eulogies of great men. The text that comes closest to a royal encomium is the praise of Pompey in Cicero's oration in favor of Manilius' law, cited above (27–49: a model encomium, according to Fronto, *On the Parthian War* 10).

Under the Roman Empire the situation changes. Encomia of mythological (or even historical) personalities were reserved for school exercises, while professional orators devoted themselves to the praise of contemporaries, the praise of emperors above all. In short, the *Evagoras* wins out over the *Encomium of Helen*. The imperial encomium, as a separate type of speech, received in Greek the name of "royal oration" (*basilikos logos*) under the empire. Menander Rhetor II puts this oratorical form at the head of his treatise to show its importance. All the official ceremonies were so many occasions for praising the emperor: imperial worship, entry into office of consuls, journeys, victory celebrations, birthdays, jubilees, weddings, funerals, contests.

Preserved examples include Roman funeral orations rewritten

by Greek historians (Appian and Cassius Dio recomposing Marcus Antonius' eulogy of Caesar, Dio redoing Tiberius' funeral oration for Augustus),[46] Pliny the Younger's *Panegyricus to Trajan*, an encomium of Philip the Arab by Pseudo–Aelius Aristides (*Oration* 35),[47] the beautiful series of Greek speeches from the fourth century AD by Libanius (*Oration* 59), Julian (*Orations* 1–2), and Themistius (*Orations* 1–19 *passim*). The Latin panegyrics inform us about the multiple circumstances in which the emperor was praised at the end of the third and in the fourth centuries: anniversaries of the founding of Rome and of Trier (2 and 7); his fifth or fifteenth regnal year (8 and 10); commemoration of his receiving the titles "Caesar" (4 and 10), "Jovius," and "Herculius" (3); expressions of gratitude (5, to Constantius on bestowing largess to the city of Autun; 8, to Constantine for visiting the city); epithalamium celebrating the marriage of Constantine and Fausta (6); victory celebration (9, on Constantine's victory over Maxentius and the expedition against the Franks); and *gratiarum actio* (11).[48]

Also to be mentioned are orations attested in the sources, but whose texts are lost: funeral orations of emperors and members of the imperial family, from Marcellus, Agrippa, Octavia, Drusus I, and Augustus to Antoninus, eulogized by Marcus Aurelius and Lucius Verus, and Pertinax, eulogized by Septimius Severus;[49] *gratiarum actiones* by Verginius Rufus for Nerva (Pliny the Younger, *Letters* 2.1.5) and Fronto for Antoninus (*Ad Antoninum imperatorem et invicem* 4.2.3); the encomia of Hadrian by Aspasius of Byblos and Orion of Alexandria; the birthday oration of Zenobius for Hadrian when Caesar; the encomium of Nicostratus for Marcus Aurelius; the epithalamium of Pollux of Naucratis for the wedding of Commodus Caesar and Crispina;[50] and the encomia of Gallienus and Aurelian by Callinicus of Petra.[51] There were also speeches on kingship (*peri basileias*) with philosophical or advisory content, represented by the speeches of Dio Chrysostom in honor of Trajan (*Orations* 1–4, 56, 62) and by the lost work of the rhetor Marcellus of Pergamum entitled *Hadrian; or, On Kingship* (*Suda* M 204).

Christian encomia in honor of the emperors baptized this tradition (e.g., Eusebius' oration honoring Constantine),[52] as did encomia of the saints, martyrs, and bishops. Orations in honor of the emperor Julian provide an eloquent example. This emperor's reign was short (two years), but it prompted, just to name the preserved texts, several speeches of Libanius, notably an address of welcome (*Oration* 13), an encomium celebrating the emperor's fourth consulate (*Oration* 12), and, after his death, a lament (*Oration* 17), as well as a funeral oration (*Oration* 18),[53] an oration of Himerius (the lost *Oration* 52), a *gratiarum actio* of the rhetor Mamertinus (*Latin Panegyrics* 11), a panegyric preserved on a recently published papyrus,[54] and, in opposition, two fierce invectives by Gregory of Nazianzus (*Orations* 4 and 5) and some hostile writing by John Chrysostom and Ephrem the Syrian.[55]

Our second example is the civic encomium. Strictly speaking, it was unknown to Classical Greek theory (Aristotle and the *Rhetoric to Alexander* omit the city as an object of praise), although praise of the city of Athens is a significant characteristic of Thucydides' *Funeral Oration* and Isocrates' *Panathenaicus*. It was embedded in other genres.[56] Hellenistic attestations are few: during this time interest in cities found expression more readily not in rhetorical encomia, but in poems and mythological, historical, and geographical studies, and in foundation legends, local histories, and travel tales, for which we have extensive fragmentary evidence. Examples from Republican Rome are also rare, apart from the Sicilian passages of Cicero cited above.

The civic encomium first appears in rhetorical theory with Quintilian (3.7.26), followed by Greek theorists during the empire (Hermogenes, *Preliminary Exercises* 7.18; Menander Rhetor I, 332, 344–365; Menander Rhetor II, 385, 387–388). Practical illustrations include Aelius Aristides' orations in honor of Athens and Rome (*Orations* 1 and 26), those of Apuleius honoring Carthage (*Florida* 18.36 and 20), Libanius' speeches in honor of Antioch (*Oration* 11), Himerius (*Oration* 41) and Themistius (*Oration* 4) celebrating Constantinople, along with numerous fragments and testimonia, as well as civic encomia found within a great number of deliberative and epideictic orations where civic encomium is not the aim, but is still an obligatory and often essential element (embassy speeches, moral and political exhortations addressed to populaces, laments for cities that were victims of natural catastrophes, speeches for arrivals or departures, and invitations).

Related to civic encomia are encomia of neighborhoods, buildings, and monuments, for example, upon the opening of recently completed edifices—a sanctuary, an aqueduct, a baths. The most frequent occasion for an encomium was the inauguration of a recently completed building, and this is exactly what we find in some of the period's speeches. The *Panegyric on the Water in Pergamum* (*Oration* 53) was written by Aelius Aristides to celebrate the commissioning of an aqueduct. Lucian's *Hippias* is dedicated to the inauguration of public baths. The sophist Polemo gave an encomium of a monument when he delivered the dedicatory speech for the temple of Olympian Zeus in Athens (the Olympieion) at the request of the emperor Hadrian (Philostratus, *Lives of the Sophists* 533):

> The temple of Olympian Zeus at Athens had been completed at last after an interval of five hundred and sixty years, and when the Emperor consecrated it as a marvellous triumph of time, he invited Polemo also to make an oration at the sacrifice. He fixed his gaze, as was his custom, on the thoughts that were already taking their place in his mind, and then flung himself into his speech, and delivered a long and admirable discourse from the base of the temple. As the prooemium of the speech he declared that not without a divine impulse was he inspired to speak on that theme. (Trans. Wright [1921:111–113])

EXPLANATION OF A CHANGE

The history of epideictic rhetoric is one of an irresistible ascension. Of secondary importance in Classical Greece and Republican Rome, and obscure in the Hellenistic era, epideictic came into its own amid the Greco-Roman world of the first centuries after Christ. During this time, the encomium was omnipresent, particularly in oratory practice (less in the theory). This development is a puzzling aspect of rhetoric, since it is both historically unexpected and intriguing. Indeed, postclassical and late antiquity has (or had) a reputation as an age of decline and fall, yet with epideictic we observe that this period, on the contrary, brought enrichment and creative growth. Paradoxically, the Imperial period turns out to be creative. In the realm of rhetoric, as in several others, the principate marked a shift, or, more precisely, a redeployment. It was the beginning of a new rhetorical world order, in which oratory served no longer to rip apart an adversary or to cow an assembly, but to spread honeyed praise and trumpet meritorious conduct with previously unparalleled frequency and variety.

The solution of the puzzle—that is, what caused this evolution—clearly lies in the political and social order. The milieu of the Greek sophists promoted epideictic. From a literary point of view, the period saw prose develop at the expense of poetry. And, above all, the major cause was the establishment of the Roman Empire, which explains the multiplication of addresses to emperors and their representatives. Furthermore, cities, especially the Greek cities belonging to the empire, developed a more aristocratic structure, which elicited encomia and other signs to honor local worthies and the cities themselves. Additionally, the imperial regime established order and peace (the famous *pax Romana*), a long-lasting stability that permitted the regular celebration of festivals, contests, and ceremonies both public and private (something that was either less common or even nonexistent before, in the Hellenistic kingdoms or at the start of the Roman conquest). It is likewise during the empire that the educational system solidified and aided rhetoric's spread.

TWO

THE GRAMMAR OF PRAISE

The intense activity, practical and theoretical, that took place during the evolution of epideictic rhetoric led to a number of technical advances. These advances focused especially on the structure and style of speeches. The ancient system of epideictic offered lists of commonplaces to be used for each sort of praised object as well as lists of different types of speeches for different occasions, aesthetic-style categories, and figures. This system, as prescribed by the theoreticians and put into practice by the orators, was in some ways a kind of "grammar" of praise, a body of rules and usage through which the speakers expressed themselves and conveyed their messages. The technique of rhetorical praise was a sort of mental equipment, which allowed everyone to recognize and to express the society's values.

THE CONCEPT OF *TOPOS*

The means of finding ideas (*inventio*, "rhetorical invention") is governed by the system of *topoi* ("commonplaces"; in Latin *loci*, and in Greek *topoi*). By definition, the orator is called upon to talk about all subjects. Therefore, he cannot rely on preexisting knowledge or specific competence in each domain given to him: what he needs is a general method that allows him to find useful ideas for every situation. The *topoi* are this method. These are not ready-made developments, or clichés, but rubrics and vantage points in the light of which the orator examines his subject.

So that the examination may be complete, the commonplaces are organized in lists meant to be exhaustive. A list of *topoi* is therefore an analytical matrix allowing the exploration of a subject from all sides. Each sector of rhetoric has its own lists: the *topoi* of the deliberative genus, the refutation, the narration, and so forth. The *topoi* are one of the most important contributions of ancient rhetoric and exerted a deep influence on European culture. For instance, Aristotelian *topoi* presented what Lawrence D. Green calls "theoretical challenges" to Renaissance translators and commentators.[1]

In accordance with this basic conception, the *topoi* of the encomium methodically organize the headings under which falls every subject that an orator is likely to have to praise. The first lists of *topoi* were developed in the Classical period of Greece for the praise of individuals. With the genus's growth, the lists multiplied, and valuable catalogues evolved for the praise of cities, gods, animals, plants, inanimate objects, and abstract ideas; these lists also became the object of philosophic reflection and sophistic refinement.

The encomiastic lists of *topoi* are notable for their targeted orientation: the succession of the *topoi* determines not only the order of the research, but also the order in which the orator will discuss the ideas discovered. In the vast majority of the theoretical texts, the succession of the *topoi* is meant to be used as a plan by the orator. The list suggests both ideas and a plan, and it is this compact, complex ensemble which the orator must learn to master and adapt. Defined in this way, the *topoi* are the indispensable framework of all rhetorical praise. This is, far and above, the subject that theoreticians studied the most scrupulously, particularly with regard to the encomia of persons.

Note that the exordium and peroration of the speech are not technically part of the lists: they are not included in the numbering of the *topoi*, and many theoreticians omit them.

THE CLASSIFICATION OF THE OBJECTS OF PRAISE

The domain of praise is universal, but not all objects are on the same level. The praise of a person enjoyed a historical and moral primacy of place: whether belonging to mythology, history, or the contemporary period, people were the first objects of praise, and humans were deemed the primary addressees for ethical approbation.

The other objects made their appearance progressively. The Greek sophists praised animals and things, which is reflected in Aristotle, who envisages the praise of gods, of animals, and of inanimate objects (*Rhetoric* 1.1366a30); but these categories are evoked only in passing, and there is no question of formulating the precepts that concern them. It is only from the beginning of the Imperial period that the multiplicity of objects is envisaged systematically. Quintilian conceives of encomia addressing a wide range of objects, of which he compiles a list and which he discusses successively (see p. 21). Hermogenes (*Preliminary Exercises* 7.14–15) and Aphthonius (*Preliminary Exercises* 8.21) compile analogous lists, which include also plants and "occasions" (*kairoi*). Menander Rhetor I also developed thorough lists for the different categories of epideictic subject (see p. 12).

The proliferation of potential praise-objects also arises from the distinction between the individual and the collective (for example, the eulogy of an Athenian and the eulogy of all the dead Athenian soldiers), and between the specific and the general (the eulogy of man in general or of Socrates, of the horse or of Pegasus, of figs or of the Damascus figs, of the sea or of the Aegean Sea).

STRUCTURE OF THE ENCOMIA OF PERSONS

The second treatise attributed to Menander Rhetor provides the best guide for studying the *topoi* for the encomia of persons. Its first two chapters (368–377) offer a full list, intended for the encomium of an emperor. This list, aside from a few details, is more complete and better structured than those left by the other theoreticians. It is a theoretical pattern, certainly, but faced with oratory practice, it shows itself to be pertinent: if there is no speech that corresponds exactly to Menander Rhetor II's *topoi*, one can simply superimpose two or three speeches to fully complete the diagram:[2]

Proem
  Difficulty of the task
  Homer and Orpheus would be needed
  Musings on where to begin
A. Origin
  Native city and nation
B. Origin
  Family
  How to cover up when subject is unfavorable
C. Birth
D. Nature
(E. Body)
F. Education
G. "Way of Being"
H. Actions
  War comes before peace, and we should divide material according to the cardinal virtues: courage in war; justice; temperance; wisdom.
I. Fortune
(J. Death)
Final comparison
Epilogue, closing with prayer

Commentary: A–B. The *topos* of "origin" comes first. It can include homeland (nation and city) and family (ancestors and parents). The most important is the family. The practice and the theory of praise of a person are evidence of this prescription.

C. The *topos* of "birth" specifies the omens, the oracles, and the dreams which accompanied the birth. Attached

> to this *topos* is a series of examples: the traditions concerning the birth of Cyrus the Elder or Romulus are recalled, which demonstrates that this *topos* was applied as a priority to sovereigns. It seems that this passage of encomium led to certain expectations on the part of the public: Menander Rhetor II (371) goes so far as to say that if the subject offers no omens or oracles of this kind, they should be invented.
>
> D. "Nature" corresponds with physical, intellectual, and moral qualities, as observed in the natural state, during the youth of the subject. Therefore, there is no overlapping with virtuous, voluntary, and considered actions accomplished in adulthood.
>
> E. Menander does not dwell on physical qualities here. The most complete list enumerates five (Aristotle, *Rhetoric* 1.1360b21–22, 1361b3–26): health; size; velocity; strength; beauty. The principal items of these are strength and beauty.

Physical qualities constituted a rich and complex subject in ancient Greece, as demonstrated by Debra Hawhee in her book *Bodily Arts*.[3] In the moralizing perspective of encomium, the body's positive qualities are native, granted to an individual by the gods or by Fortune as a last resort; they deserve to be praised only if they manifest some virtue. Beauty is seen to be like a mirror and a peril where the virtues of the soul are revealed.

Even if all ages can have their own physical qualities, the praise of physical qualities, as a *topos*, has its place at the beginning of the encomium, because physical qualities principally correspond with youth. Therefore, the center of the speech is dedicated to just moral qualities.

> F. "Education" is the first item which directly brings intellectual and moral qualities into play. Theoreticians divide it into two sections: care in early childhood, and then upbringing more generally.[4] This category inaugurates an examination of the soul that will be continued in the fol-

lowing *topoi*. The learning years play a central role in the definition of a person. Education is received from outside, but the profit the child gains from it, the way he distinguishes himself from his peers, gives evidence of his intellectual and moral qualities. Such qualities are of central interest to the encomiast.

G. The concept of "way of being" (in Greek, *epitēdeumata*) corresponds, according to the authors, to two distinct matters. In its first meaning, it is the chosen way of life, the career embraced since the person's youth, for example the career of soldiering, of athleticism, or of philosophy. In its second meaning, it is the conduct, the way of being, the habits of the soul; it relates to a moral portrait, applicable prior to accomplished actions; for example, character traits such as gentleness, sociability, or moderation would be praised.[5]

H. The *topos* "actions" combines the actions accomplished by the person and the virtues that these actions manifest. This is the crucial issue, on which more will be said below.

I. The *topos* "fortune" brings together the benefits granted by fate or by Fortune. This is a question of inserting *in fine* those exterior goods received over the course of the life that had no place in the rest of the list, such as success, children, friends, and the like. Seen from the perspective of luck and divine favor, these goods become worthy of congratulations and even praise, especially if the orator emphasizes that the subject has made good use of them. This is the occasion to revisit the biography which has just been outlined, but from a different angle—this is a summarizing function.

J. "Death" for obvious reasons only has a place in the funeral oration. This *topos*, which is not presented in Menander's pattern, discusses the death itself; what followed it, funeral competition, oracles, illustration of the descendants; the divine honors, the decrees, the statues, even the survival of the intellectual powers through literary works.[6]

Menander Rhetor II's list, which seems so simple and balanced, is in reality the result of centuries of reflection on rhetorical and philosophical problems.

The first Greek rhetorical eulogies, the public funeral orations (*epitaphioi*), followed a chronological plan. They narrated the development and the exploits of this collective person that constituted the Athenians. Faced with this narrative tradition, Greek rhetoric in the fifth century BC included "pure portraits," which described the qualities of a person without a chronology: such is the case for the encomia made by Adrastus in Euripides' *Suppliant Women* (860–908), and similarly the preserved fragment of the funeral oration of Gorgias enumerates the virtues of those citizens who died for the homeland. The "portrait" is a second potential model for the rhetorical praise of an individual. It does not have the simplicity of the chronological order, but it responds to an ethical demand for the ordering of goods and virtues.

Rhetorical praise has sampled these possibilities. For example, Isocrates adopted the chronological plan in his encomia of Alcibiades (*On the Team of Horses* 25–41) and of Helen (*Encomium of Helen* 16–66). But in the *Panegyricus* he made an effort to articulate in sections the succession of the Athenians' actions. The actions are reviewed in chronological order, but are divided into the categories of "peaceful deeds" (26–50) and "military exploits" (51–99); for peaceful deeds, a division into domains is introduced: politics, commerce, religious festivals, culture, intellectual achievements. Finally, in the eulogy of Evagoras, Isocrates attempted a mixed form, which was as much a narrative as a portrait (*Evagoras* 12–72):

Ancestors (12–18)
Homeland (19–20)
Birth (21)
Childhood (22)
    Physical and moral qualities
Adulthood, up to coming to power (23–40)
    Physical and moral qualities

Actions: exile, return to the homeland, and coming to power

Comparison

The reign (41–64)

Qualities of the king

His actions

General comparison (65–69)

Blessing (70–72)

Most notable is the alternation, within a globally biographical schema, between synthetic passages describing the person's character at each stage of his life and narrative accounts of the actions in the period in question. The *Evagoras* reconciles description and narrative through the means of an elegant pulsation between ethical passages and historical passages.

It was assumed, from the time of the Classical Greek period, that rhetorical praise should take into account the principal stages of life, from birth to the present day—until death, when a funeral oration would be made—but the organization of the central section, corresponding to adulthood, remained open: between narrative and portrait, all combinations were attempted, under the form of juxtaposition, alternation, or fusion. The meaning of these exploratory attempts goes beyond a simple question of plan, as they represent the creation of a new literary genre, which took shape by borrowing from ethical and philosophical analyses and from the chronological methods of historians. In this process, the very image of the human person was at stake. What is a man? A man is what he does: the orator must recount the exploits accomplished. But moral philosophy proposes that merits be judged: a man is what he is worth. The birth of rhetorical praise in ancient Greece was dominated by this dialogue between chronological narrative and moral evaluation.

The schema that became dominant, as seen in Menander Rhetor II's work, represents a fusion of evaluative and narrative approaches. Rhetorical encomium resembles both portrait and biography, while still distinguishing itself from these two forms.

Like portrait, it analyzes qualities, but still tries to follow the person from his birth to the present day. Like biography, it narrates a life and paints a character, but in a different spirit. Biography is more narrative. It is closer to the historical facts, more attentive to the details, to psychological particularities, while encomium, in comparison, tends toward abstraction and stylization.

Praise is about "goods." According to traditional Greek conceptions, its focus is the "qualities" of the object (*ta prosonta* or *ta huparkhonta*). These qualities are "the goods" (*ta agatha*), or, combining two phrases, "the goods pertaining to the object" (*ta prosonta agatha, ta huparkhonta agatha*). If we consider the list of the canonized definitions of rhetorical encomium, we see the recurrence of just these notions: all of these definitions have the commonality of placing the notion of "goods" at the heart of the encomium. For instance, in Isocrates (*Encomium of Helen* 12) the orator is told

> to discuss subjects that are commonly agreed to be good or noble or excelling in *aretē* ["virtue, moral worth"]. (Trans. Mirhady [Mirhady and Too 2000:35])

Aelius Theon (*Exercises* 9[8].109) states:

> Encomion is language revealing the greatness of virtuous actions and other good qualities belonging to a particular person. (Trans. Kennedy [2003:50])

If praise is about goods, it is necessary, in the interest of correctly praising the object, to know what the real goods are, a question which requires a detour to the philosophers. Ancient philosophy highlighted a three-way division of goods: goods of the soul, goods of the body, and exterior goods (e.g., Plato, *Laws* 3.697b, 5.743e; Aristotle, *Nicomachean Ethics* 1.1098b12–16; Aristotle, *Politics* 7.1323a25–26). Throughout Classical antiquity this division of goods into three hierarchical categories continued to be a widely adopted idea, as Epictetus observes (3.7.2):

> Now that three things belong to man, soul, and body, and things external, hardly anyone denies. (Trans. Oldfather [1925–1928:2.49])

The problem of the epideictic list of *topoi* was thus envisaged in the ethical framework of the tripartite division of goods: birth, education, richness, power, success (exterior goods); then beauty, health, and other physical qualities (bodily goods); and finally virtues and virtuous actions (goods of the soul). This underlying classification is important in encomium. Menander Rhetor II's plan, as seen before, complies with this tenet and offers a formula suited to tackling ethical demands:

A–D. Exterior goods
E. Bodily goods
F–H. Goods of the soul
I–J. Exterior goods

The problem of physical or exterior goods enjoyed by the person throughout his existence is tackled by the importance which the plan accords Fortune at the end of the speech; this *topos* allows for a recapitulation of all the individual's goods, without disrupting the chronological order.

As for the central part of the encomium, the main problem lay in the connection between actions and virtues. Again, this was a philosophical issue. Beginning with Aristotle (*Rhetoric* 1.1367b27–28), actions, in epideictic theory, were considered to be subordinate to virtues:

> Praise is speech that makes clear the greatness of virtue [of the subject praised]. There is thus need to show that actions have been of that sort. (Trans. Kennedy [1991:84])

The link between actions and virtues is indeed essential to Aristotelian ethics: virtue is, by definition, the producer of great actions, and inversely, we judge the value of a man through his acts—providing these are intentional acts, resulting from a choice, which excludes success resulting from fortune. Aristotle's input was one of theorizing upon, and discussing the consequences of, this link for rhetorical praise. As virtues constituted the *quod erat demonstrandum*, it was logical to give them the role of guiding principle; actions functioned as clues or proofs. Aristotle's lesson has not been forgotten, and actions are generally presented, in ancient epideictic rhetoric, as the manifestation of the virtues of the *laudandus*. Theorists and orators often adopt the combination of virtues and actions in favor of the former: the person's actions are ordered according to the principal virtues, or qualities, he has shown and the domains in which he has excelled. The opposite combination (virtues subordinate to actions, that is to say, the description of the actions in a chronological order) is rarer; there are instances of it in the Latin panegyrics, starting with that of Pliny the Younger.

The inner architecture of the *topos* of actions/virtues consists of the classification of virtues, a classification that was the object, in the philosophical tradition, of numerous and varied discussions. Another digression to ethics is necessary here, in order to draw out the elements used directly in the encomium.

Plato, in his mature dialogues, enumerates the four parts of virtue: "prudence" or "intelligence," "moderation, temperance," "justice," and "courage";[7] "piety," which formed a fifth virtue in the *Protagoras*, lost its autonomy to become, in this tetrad, a component of "justice."[8] This classification became dominant and the rhetorical encomia adopted it, as Plato himself recognized. Agatho's speech in praise of Love (*Symposium* 196b–d) slavishly follows this fourfold division:

> Enough has now been said, though much remains unsaid, of the beauty of our god; next shall Love's goodness [*aretē*] be my theme. The strongest plea for this is that neither to a god he gives nor from a god receives any injury, nor from men receives it nor to men gives it. . . . Then, over and above his justice [*dikaiosunē*], he is richly endowed with temperance [*sōphrosunē*]. . . . And observe how in valour [*andreia*] "not even the God of War withstands" Love. . . . So much for justice and

temperance and valour in the god: it remains to speak of skill [*sophia*]. (Trans. Lamb [1925:157])

Theorists of encomium, like the orators, used this most simple and widely known division of virtues—which they themselves proliferated further, as indicated by the appearance of this list in school curricula.[9]

In its simplicity, the list of the virtues brings some serious philosophical problems to the surface, without claiming to resolve them. We expected rhetorical theory to fix an order, and as such a hierarchy, for the four listed virtues. And yet this question, deemed so important by Plato and Aristotle, is almost never addressed in rhetoric. Each theorist, each orator, adopts a different order. An absolute hierarchy is renounced in favor of isolated preferences influenced by conjectural criteria: the usefulness of the demonstration and the sequence of the sections of the speech. Moreover, rhetoric did not take up the Socratic doctrine of unity of virtue, or the Stoic concept of interdependence between virtues. It rather highlights the distinction between virtues. This plurality is in line with the common conception, already defended by Isocrates (*Encomium of Helen* 1).

Sometimes a further distinction is made between those actions accomplished during war and those actions accomplished during peace. This is a classic division in encomium that can be found in the *Panegyricus* of Isocrates and the *Panegyricus* of Pliny, who successively praise wartime exploits and peaceful actions. As a general rule, this distinction is applied to the encomia of statesmen. When the war/peace dichotomy is present, it is the dominant factor, as in Menander Rhetor II's schema, and the different virtues are inserted into one or the other, and sometimes in one and the other, of these two sections.

An important, if often neglected, stage in the history of the epideictic *topoi* is the list of a "person's attributes" (Gk. *ta parakolouthounta tōi prosōpōi*; Lat. *personis attributae res*). This list's primary application is in the theory of judicial argumentation: to examine the life and the personality of the accused, the rhetoricians propose a series of sections that define the person and allow one to find arguments concerning his innocence or guilt. For instance, if it is the case that the accused denied having committed the crime, the defense will make particular recourse to the examination of will and of power, showing that a certain act does not correspond with the accused's condition, character, or means. An analogous examination can be applied to all the people involved, and even the witnesses. A full list of the attributes of persons is given in Cicero (*On Invention* 1.34–36):

- Name
- Nature
  - Sex, race, place of birth, family, age
- Manner of life
  - Education, friends, profession, home life
- Fortune
  - Slave or free, rich or poor . . . , children, nature of his death
- Habit
  - Stable and absolute constitution of mind or body
- Feeling
  - Temporary change in mind or body, interests, purposes
- Achievements, accidents, speeches made
  - What he did, what happened to him, what he said

In that it involves analyzing the notion of person, this list responds to the same preoccupations which feature in the epideictic genre. The list of a person's attributes is an innovation of the Hellenistic period; it likely was influenced by the epideictic genre. Then, by cross-fertilization, it was able to influence rhetorical encomium.[10]

The epideictic *topoi* evolved into a general and accepted doctrine. Whether subject to approval or criticism, the list of the *topoi* emerged as a reference point. The problems posed during the Classical period progressively received convergent or similar solutions, while the content of each *topos* was specified and systematized. Begun during the Hellenistic period, this process came to an end in the age of the Second Sophistic: from Cicero to Menander Rhetor, we see the realization of an epideictic conception of the human person.

The *topoi* of rhetorical praise in fact lead to an implicit anthropology, which comes down to a few essential traits. From birth to death, the pattern follows a biographical order: excellence is inscribed in the timeline of life. Simultaneously, from the perspective of the classification of goods, it is a deepening, which proceeds from the exterior (birth) toward the body (physical qualities), then from the body to the soul (education, way of being, virtues), with Fortune and death forming a sort of conclusion. This deepening implies a hierarchy: the exterior and physical goods are not indifferent, but it is virtue that counts. So, the *topoi* come back to philosophical notions, but presented in a simplified form, linked to observations of good sense, and organized into a list, in line with the demands of the rhetorical method.

The *topoi* of rhetorical praise provided a preeminent model, one which played an important role in ancient thinking in very distant periods and places. All that remained was to extend this model by elaborating similar outlines for the other objects of encomium.

HOW TO PRAISE CITIES

Analogy is important in passing from one category of objects to another. To praise any object whatsoever, the *topoi* for the encomium of a person are employed, by means of a simple analogical transposition, which replaces, for example, the parents with the founder (in the case of a city) or the inventor (in the case of a thing). This principle is unique to encomium, and it reflects the history of the epideictic genus itself: confronted with the multiplication of the objects of praise, the theoreticians used the reference point of the human person, which was the primitive object—and they were helped in this by the ancient habits of anthropomorphism and personification. So Quintilian (*The Orator's Education* 3.7.26):

> Cities are praised on similar lines to men. The founder stands for the father. . . . The virtues and vices seen in actions are the same as with individuals, the only special features being those

which come from the site and the fortifications. (Trans. Russell [2001:2.115])

From Aristotle to the beginning of the Imperial period, rhetorical theory did not study the encomium of the city. In Aristotle's *Rhetoric*, the *Rhetoric to Alexander*, the *Rhetoric to Herennius*, and the rhetorical treatises of Cicero, the city is not one of the objects of encomium. The theoreticians study only the topographical description, for example in the preliminary exercise "description of place" (*ekphrasis topou*): this exercise is present in all of the Greek *progymnasmata*.[11]

The *topoi* for encomia of cities appeared in the Latin domain with Quintilian, who offers a tripartite plan in but a few lines: founder, virtues manifested by the actions, topographical site (*The Orator's Education* 3.7.26, above). The Greek theorists lag behind the Latin theorists: it is not until Hermogenes' *Progymnasmata* and then the treatises of Pseudo–Dionysius of Halicarnassus and the two Menander Rhetors that a complete theory of praise of cities can be found. The practice of the orators, notably Dio Chrysostom and Aelius Aristides, reveals that the Greeks knew, from the end of the first century AD, a schema parallel to Quintilian's. Dio, writing an encomium of Nicaea (*Orations* 39.2), distinguishes precisely Quintilian's three points: origin of the city; beauty of the territory, agricultural production, and population figures; finally, the virtues. Aelius Aristides regularly applies *topoi* which return to these three fundamental elements (*Orations* 1, 17, 27). These clues seem then to suggest that the emergence of the topic of encomium of cities took place some time in the first century AD: precisely the period when documentation begins to give evidence of an assiduous practice of encomia of cities, notably because of the renaissance of the Greek towns in the Roman Empire. This emergence of the *topoi* constitutes not a birth born of nothing but the ordering of preexisting elements (found in works by geographers, historians, philosophers, etc.). These elements were melded into one whole, which, as such, became new.

Quintilian's schema (quoted above) involves distinguishing between two categories of *topoi*: on one hand, those analogically borrowed from the encomium of an individual, that is to say, the founder, which takes the place of the father, and virtues, which are the same as those for a person; and on the other, the specific *topoi* (*illa propria*, Quintilian says), which are drawn from topography. Pseudo-Dionysius' and Menander's schemata reflect the same doctrine.[12]

The theoretical list of *topoi* may be summarized as follows (the actual practice was more flexible):

• *Situation and site.* It is necessary to make an initial distinction between the "situation" or "position" (*thesis*) and the "site" (*phusis*) of the city. Ancient geographers knew these concepts[13] and modern geographers still use them: the situation of a town is defined through its relationship with the whole region, while the site corresponds to its exact location. This *topos* includes, for the situation, the position of the place in relation to the earth, the sea, and the sky (orientation and climate); for the site, the nature of the place, envisaged from the point of view of the relief, the hydrographic conditions and the vegetation (Menander Rhetor I, 344–345; Menander Rhetor II, 384).

• *Origin.* Menander Rhetor I (353–359) offers a detailed study of the origin (*genos*) of the city. He deconstructs this *topos* into five parts: founder, population, period of foundation, occasion from which the city resulted (colonization, synoecism, transfer, etc.), and cause of the foundation.

• *Education, political regime, way of being.* In these *topoi* the personification of the city is revealed.

• *Actions and virtues.* This *topos* is governed by the same ethical conceptions as those in the encomium of a person. Actions are the manifestation of virtues: therefore the architecture of the *topos* consists of a tetrad, already analyzed, of justice, temperance, prudence, and courage (Quintilian 3.7.26; Menander Rhetor I, 361–365; Menander Rhetor II, 385–386).

• *Edifices and beauties.* This *topos* includes temples, sanctuaries, and sacred woods, then harbors, porticos, acropolises, agora, roads and avenues, and finally thermal baths, fountains, ramparts, theaters, gymnasiums, statues, and, occasionally, paintings or libraries. In line with the conception of the praise of a city as a collective praise, private houses are rarely evoked. Nothing is said of workshops, factories, and the like. Aqueducts receive special attention in pleas to the emperor, because water services are considered to be a topic of particular interest to Roman authorities (Menander Rhetor II, 423).

This list of *topoi* supposes a sort of personification of the city. The city has not only a soul and a biography, but also a body, consisting of its constructions, its site, and its location. Here we encounter a moral conundrum, which mirrors that arising from the encomium of a person: Is it legitimate to praise the physical reality of the city? Is it legitimate to praise material goods? Such questions, often debated in rhetorical encomia to cities, indicate the weight of ethical concerns in the epideictic topic.

The response is as follows: in the beauty of the sites and buildings, the grandeur of virtues and actions can be perceived. The challenge is to discern the marks of past worth in the current state of the territory and the city, for they attest to moral qualities. Sanctuaries, for instance, express the piety of the city. The landscape, like buildings, takes on moral qualities.

HOW TO PRAISE A GOD

Rhetorical treatises highlight that the praise of the gods has a special name: it is to be called not "praise" (*epainos* or *enkōmion*), but "hymn" (*humnos*).[14] The noun *humnos* and the verb *humnein* are the terms employed to refer to rhetorical encomia to the gods. This word indicates a link to poetry.

The chronological distribution of the rhetorical sources here is comparable to that of the sources for the encomium of a city. The only remaining texts from the Classical and Hellenistic periods are Plato's *Symposium* and the inscription known as the "aretalogy of Maroneia";[15] the mythological figures praised by the First

Sophistic and later in the *progymnasmata* hark back to the encomium of a person and not to the encomium of a god. The theory of the hymn begins, for us, with Quintilian, and the corresponding Greek treatises are later: notably those of Alexander, son of Numenius, and Menander Rhetor I.[16] In practice, the Aristidian collection is the primary source.[17]

The rhetorical hymn, aside from variations specific to each work, consists of three principal *topoi*: the nature of the god (*phusis*); his birth (*genos*), including his age or his antiquity; and finally, the essential *topos* of the powers (*dunameis*), which includes actions (*erga*) and inventions (*heurēmata*) in which these powers are manifest. This last *topos* comes with a series of adjoining themes which once more express power and divine functions: cult, name, epithets, relationships with the other gods, children. Here, for instance, is the treatment of the matter in the fragment by Alexander, son of Numenius (in Spengel 1853–1856:3.4–6):

Nature
Birth
Honors, cult
Power, inventions, actions, kind deeds
Relations with other gods

The list of *topoi* of the rhetorical hymn would appear to be a systemization into three main sections ("nature," "birth," "power") of an image of divinity that originates from common belief, poetic hymns, and the influence of the philosophers. The analogy with the encomium of man also played a role: in both cases there is a *topos* of birth, and the divine powers manifest in the god's deeds recall the *topos* of the actions/virtues. The hymn also includes, as do the encomia of people and towns, a *topos* of "nature"—although this word takes on a different meaning in each case. Among the most important adjoining themes figures the name, which can have a place—albeit rarely—in the praise of a person, and the cult, which is comparable to the honors received (for example the honors received from the emperor) for a man or a town. These similarities can be explained through the traces of anthropomorphic conception of divinity. There are nonetheless differences separating the two patterns (encomium of a person and encomium of a god), one being ethical and biographical, and the other theological. The main *topoi* are the following:

- *Nature.* The *topos* of "nature" is regularly positioned at the beginning of the encomium. In Quintilian (3.7.7), this *topos* discusses the nature of the divine in general. In other cases, it discusses the nature of the specific god to whom the encomium is dedicated (for example, the praise of Poseidon in Aelius Aristides, *Orations* 46.5–7: the nature of this god is the humid element). This *topos* is often considered to have a philosophical character, which may be too pronounced for orators and for their audience.

- *Birth.* In line with the use of hymns and poetic prayers, the rhetorical hymn evokes the birth of the god by making reference to mythological information: for example, whether this god is a descendant of Zeus, or if he is ancient (Quintilian 3.7.7–8; Alexander 5). The miracles accompanying the birth are not omitted: for example, the birth of Athena, the conception of Heracles, the gestation of Dionysus (Aristides, *Orations* 37.2–3; 40.2; 41.3).

- *Power and kind deeds.* "Power" includes the sphere of action of the god and the spatial representation of the divine strength; it is the "empire" of the god. Then can be found the god's inventions and the arts over which he presides. Finally, the actions are evoked, such as mythological episodes, or permanent activity. Divine actions are kind deeds: they are classed according to their beneficiaries, distinguishing actions towards the other gods, actions towards men, and eventually actions towards animals, plants, places (Alexander 6).

- *Adjoining themes.* The "honors" the god enjoys cover the cult he receives from either all or the best people. One can also describe the relationship between the praised god and the other gods, and cite his names and appellations. Gods have numerous names. A special connection with the gods may be obtained through the knowledge of their names, and the nomination is a means of making contact with the divine.[18]

HOW TO PRAISE ANIMALS AND INANIMATE OBJECTS

Regarding animals and inanimate objects, the situation is varied and several formulas are proposed.

The analogy with the encomium of people is evident in the encomium of animals, or even plants: orators praise the place where the plants originate, equivalent to homeland, and the god to whom they are consecrated, which takes the place of parents; their growth can then be described (as a substitute for education), as can their aspect (as a substitute for physical qualities); in place of virtues, notions of utility will be brought into play, and finally, those of charm (Hermogenes, *Preliminary Exercises* 17–18, 19).

A particularly common list of *topoi* for the praise of objects is (cf. Quintilian, *The Orator's Education* 3.7.27):

Creator
Beauty
Utility

Another method of praising an art, an activity, or a virtue consists of transferring the encomium to the person who practices it. Hermogenes does this, drawing the encomium of hunting back to its inventors (Artemis and Apollo), to those who used it first (the heroes), and to its everyday users (the hunters of the current time), whose physical and moral qualities will be examined (*Preliminary Exercises* 17).

Finally, an object may be praised as if it were divine; the divinization of the object involves using the topic of the hymn. Such is the case of an encomium of Law by Dio Chrysostom (*Orations* 75) or of the Aegean Sea by Aelius Aristides (*Orations* 44).

CONCLUSION TO THE *TOPOI*

The multiplicity of the *topoi* is proof of the importance of the encomiastic schemes in ancient thinking. The basis is formed of the anthropological list, which is the oldest and most discussed, and then, in the post-Classical period, the other schemes were elaborated, representing a progressive enrichment of the epideictic universe. The lists of *topoi* build bridges between the authors, such as between Isocrates and Pseudo-Aristides, Aristotle and Aelius Theon, and Lucian and Quintilian.

These ancient "commonplace" investigations had significant consequences, because in each instance they presumed an analysis of the object. The rhetorical lists of *topoi* present models of excellence, which combine facts—biography, description, history, mythology—with moral, social, theological, and aesthetic values. The *topoi* of the personal encomium presume a conception of humanity, an implied anthropology, and a reflection on the virtues and on the criteria of human action. Likewise, the *topoi* of the civic encomium presume a composite vision of the city in its geographical, historical, and political aspects. The *topoi* of the divine encomium presume mythological and theological beliefs. By choosing and ordering themes, by establishing the grammar of the encomium, rhetors voiced and wrote down prevailing conceptions sincerely held and widely shared. Epideictic rhetoric thus wrote a not-negligible chapter in the intellectual and cultural history of the ancient world.

This is why we can characterize the lists of *topoi* as reference schemes, duly elaborated, specified, and articulated, and respectable and efficient analytical frameworks, which enabled the ancient encomiast to perceive objects clearly and to appreciate their merits equitably. Only when misused did the *topoi* become superficial, routine, bookish, such as when they were simply reused in a servile and mechanical manner.

Good use of the *topoi*, on the contrary, required:

- *Examining*. The orator examines his subject in the light of the lists of *topoi*, and ideas are born of precisely this contact between the framework for analysis and the point of its application.

• *Specifying.* Since the list of *topoi* gathers together only general categories, it is up to the orator to add to this what the theorist is unable to foresee: the traits specific to the object, both its singular and its eminent merits, while making an effort to adapt it.

• *Choosing.* The orator must choose and edit. The examination undertaken through the means of the *topoi* indeed suggests a large number of ideas: so, it is necessary to act with discrimination, to avoid being too lengthy, and especially to retain only the strongest of the points, the ideas relevant to the demonstration, the qualities really deserving of praise. One must know both how to speed up and how to omit.

THE TYPOLOGY OF SPEECHES

Thus far we have discussed pure encomium, devoted to just one subject and composed independently of the conditions in which it would be presented. But epideictic eloquence very much takes into account "circumstances," the famous *kairos* whose importance we are aware of from the beginnings of Greek rhetoric, in the First Sophistic and in the work of the founding fathers of Greek praise, Pindar, Gorgias, and Isocrates.[19] As we have seen in chapter 1, the multiplication of occasional speeches was one of the major innovations of epideictic rhetoric during the Imperial period. When encomium responds to a given situation, it must be specified: on the one hand is pure and simple encomium, common to all circumstances, general and abstract; on the other is specified discourse, which follows diverse modalities, according to the demands of the subject. For example, the praise of a governor is a pure "encomium," but if this encomium is given in precise circumstances, like the welcoming of the magistrate, its content changes and it becomes a "welcome speech" (*prosphōnētikos*). This involves adapting the encomiastic structure to the occasion of the speech; to refer to this procedure, we propose to use the word "typology," in the sense of distinguishing between the different types of speeches.

The most complete typology appears in Menander Rhetor II, as shown by the table of contents of his treatise *On Epideictic Speeches*:[20]

The Imperial Oration

The Speech of Arrival

The Talk

The Propemptic Talk (Valediction)

The Epithalamium

The Bedroom Speech

The Birthday Speech

The Consolatory Speech

The Address

The Funeral Speech

The Crown Speech

The Ambassador's Speech

The Speech of Invitation

The Leavetaking

The Monody

The Sminthiac Oration (In Honor of Apollo Smintheus)

These different types of epideictic orations emerge from a process of combination, consisting of associating distinct subjects in the same speech, for example, a man and a city, a god and a monument. Starting with a small number of basic elements (praise of an official, a city, a god, etc.), and combining them, the orator will be able to produce any number of orations answering to the necessities of every situation. The simplest form associates multiple speeches of personal praise: for example, in the welcoming address to honor a governor arriving in his province, the encomium of the governor is always preceded by an encomium of the emperor who dispatched this official to his grateful subjects. The next combination, which is very frequent, associates praise of an individual and praise of a city: the farewell addressed to an individual who is leaving on a journey contains, with praise of the voyager, a praise of the city he is departing. Epideictic oratory similarly entertains associating praise of the gods with praise of the places consecrated to them. In public or private ceremonies, epideictic oratory unites praise of persons and praise of the ceremony itself: thus, the different types of wedding oration join praise of the married couple with praise of marriage.

The associative method achieves its final pinnacle in the "panegyric" (*panēgyrikos logos*), a solemn and complex oration in which there is praise for the god to whom the panegyric is dedicated; for the city where it is taking place, with attention, perhaps, to the sanctuary and statue; for the festival itself; for the emperor; and possibly for the organizers of the contest. In its strictest sense, "panegyric discourse" (or, if specifying which festival is being discussed, "Olympic discourse," "Panathenaic discourse," etc.) refers in the Imperial period to a speech given during a "festival" (*panēgyris*), and has the function of praising the festival and everything relating to it, notably the city where it is celebrated and the god to whom it is dedicated. This is where the innovations begin, because the content of the "panegyric discourse" changed after the Classical period: it was no longer a deliberative discourse giving advice about Greece's interests, but rather a speech wholly becoming of the epideictic genre.

Encomium is therefore the guiding principle of the panegyrics by Aelius Aristides and of the instructions relative to this type of speech by Pseudo-Dionysius and Menander Rhetor II:

Aristides, *Orations* 27: *Panegyric in Cyzicus*

Praise of Cyzicus

Praise of the Temple of Hadrian

Praise of the emperors Marcus Aurelius and Lucius Verus

Aristides, *Orations* 46: *The Isthmian Oration*

Praise of Poseidon

Praise of Corinth

Praise of the Isthmian Festival

Praise of Leucothea and Palaemon

Pseudo–Dionysius of Halicarnassus, *Rhetoric* 1.255–260: *Panegyrics*

Praise of the god

Praise of the city

Praise of the festival

Praise of the crown

Praise of the emperor

Praise of the organizers

Menander Rhetor II, *Division of Epideictic Speeches* 437–446: *The Sminthiac Oration*

Praise of Apollo

Praise of Alexandria Troas

Praise of festival

Praise of temple and statue

Another kind of epideictic typology treats the expression of feelings and passions. Here the basis of the speech is still encomium, be it singular or multiple, conducted according to the listing of the *topoi*. But an emotional tone is added, occurring, according to the particular situation, in three distinct ways:

- The addition can be confined to the exordium and the peroration.

- Sometimes it takes the form of a supplementary chapter, entirely dedicated to the expression of an emotion that defines the specific aim of the speech.

- It is often interwoven and mixed with the encomium, in the form of an oft-repeated idea or feeling.

The most frequent emotions are gratitude, affection, joy, and sadness. This emotion set can be detected in Menander Rhetor's treatises, which include, in addition to pure praise and blame, wishes and prayers, consolations, thanks, descriptions, and the expression of multiple feelings. The importance ascribed to these annex forms is characteristic of the Imperial era; without displacing the central role of praise in the epideictic genus, the forms enrich the definition of the genus.

The speeches of thanks, for instance the *gratiarum actio* of the consuls, are meant to express gratitude (see Pliny the Younger, *Panegyricus* 90–93, 95; *Latin Panegyrics* 11.15–32). The typical plan for this oratorical form envisages the new consul thanking the emperor first on behalf of everyone, and then on his own part and that of his colleague. The first section consists of a pure encomium of the emperor. The second section expresses gratitude through a range of means. The orator proclaims his debt and expresses his joy. He describes and amplifies the favor he is receiving, its importance, its honorific character, opposing the present state of things to the miseries suffered under the previous—bad—emperor, or to the sinful regime of the accession to the former consulate. He even speaks of himself, of his qualification to receive this honor that he has not solicited. Finally, he gives assurances that he will prove himself worthy of the favor and vows to undertake projects for the future.

An example of affection is provided by the invitation speech, addressed to a governor to invite him to visit a city (Menander Rhetor II, 424–425, 428). The orator makes an encomium of the governor, giving it an emotional coloring. He affirms that the city desires the presence of the governor, and that the governor wishes to visit the city; if the governor has already visited and is being invited for a second visit, the governor and the city become two separated lovers who are eager to see one another once more. Apuleius employs the words *amor* and *desiderium* to qualify Carthage's attachment to its proconsul (*Florida* 9.31, 32, 34, 37).

Joy is expressed frequently in ceremony eloquence, for example in marriage speeches, birthday speeches, and panegyrics.

The primary place for sadness is the funeral oration. From the time of the Athenian *epitaphios*, this oratory form combined four elements: praise, lamentation, consolation, exhortation. Lamentation is the proper place for pathos. In time lamentation, under the name of "monody" (*monōidia*), became an autonomous speech (Menander Rhetor II, 434–437). Rhetorical lamentation also spread to Rome. In his funeral oration of Julius Caesar, according to certain sources, Marcus Antonius used this trick, contrary to the usage of the *laudatio funebris*, by ending his eulogy to Caesar with a lamentation aimed at stirring up the people's pity and anger.[21] The epideictic rhetoric of the Imperial period can be seen to have developed the expression of the pathetic, in the context of a funeral oration and in the form of an autonomous speech, in respect to both a person (deceased) and a city (destroyed by a natural disaster). Here, epideictic rhetoric was inspired by the *topoi* of pity and of indignation, which were used in other sectors of rhetoric (the *ēthopoiia* of the *progymnasmata*, some judicial and deliberative speeches).[22] It was also inspired by poetic tradition.

Finally let us mention the most informal of all speeches, called *lalia* ("talk") or *prolalia* ("preliminary talk"),[23] and the whole subject of letters of recommendation, which belongs to all periods and has close connections with praise.[24]

THE EPIDEICTIC STYLES

Not only structure but also style reflects the development of epideictic rhetoric. In the Classical era of Greece, the theorists required of the encomium an elaborate, studied style anxious to please, featuring literary references as well as the use of Gorgianic figures and the periodicity Isocrates favored. This conception of epideictic style is enshrined in Isocrates and Aristotle.[25]

With the development of epideictic rhetoric, though, style diversified. Prompting this diversification was a series of principles that defined the proper use of style—or rather, styles—in oratory. First of all, the accomplished orator must know how to handle all styles and employ them at will. Next, he must adapt form to matter: the multiplication of types of orations requires entertaining different styles within the epideictic genus, in order to respond to the diversity of situations. Finally, the orator must vary the style from one passage to another within the same speech, in order to avoid boredom and to attain each of his appointed goals. For all these reasons, the conception of epideictic style had to be enriched. That is why theoreticians such as Pseudo–Dionysius of Halicarnassus, Menander Rhetor I, and Menander Rhetor II approved in the encomium:

- the elegant style, in the manner of Isocrates, characterized by a search for formal beauty, parallelisms, and antitheses;

- the politically charged and contentious, comparable to the styles used in deliberative and judicial speeches;

- grandeur and majesty, notably with regard to the gods and key historical or mythological subjects;

- simplicity and gentleness, with no flourishes, as suits narrative sections or speeches for private ceremonies;

- sheer virtuosity and Asianism (a term that designates the most artificial types of prose style), both very appreciated by the sophists.[26]

In actual practice, epideictic writing became more supple. It used diverse aesthetic means in the service of diverse rhetorical tasks, for example, of composing an exalted hymn, a solemn or charming address, a witty introduction, a sorrowful lament, or a frightening account.

The stylistic dimension was very important in antiquity. To fully appreciate this, it would be necessary for us to examine the texts close-up, in the original language, studying precise passages, an endeavor that is beyond the scope of the present book.

TROPES AND FIGURES

In addition to the major stylistic trends, as enumerated above, the epideictic styles are distinguished by certain isolated and characteristic tropes and figures, three in particular: apostrophe, hyperbole, and comparison/metaphor.

Apostrophe, which "is 'turning away' from the normal audience . . . and the addressing of another, second audience, surprisingly chosen by the orator,"[27] is a figure of thought that appears often in judicial and deliberative eloquence. The beginning of Cicero's *First Catilinarian* is a well-known example: "In heaven's name, Catiline, how long will you take advantage of our forbearance?" (trans. MacDonald [1976:33]). This figure was developed over time in epideictic eloquence; of little note in the Classical period, it took on more importance in the Imperial period with the development of the genre.

The most marked case is that of the apostrophe to the deceased in funeral oration.[28] In this context, it works to reinforce the pathetic character of the lamentations. Accompanied by the appropriate *actio*, this figure always produces a striking effect, as those who heard André Malraux's famous peroration know:

> As Leclerc entered the Invalides with his cortège of honour from the hot suns of Africa and the battles of Alsace, enter now, Jean Moulin, with your terrible cortège. (Speech to mark the transfer of Jean Moulin's ashes to the Panthéon, in Malraux 1971:135)

When the encomium is not a funeral eulogy, the orator can, in the same way, directly apostrophize the object being praised—god or man. This is another characteristic use in the Imperial period. In the hymn, these apostrophes appear in the invocations contained in the exordium and the peroration, which frame the body of the speech, composed in the third person. Already known by poets, the direct double greeting, at the beginning and the end, is common in Aelius Aristides' hymns (*Orations* 37, 38, 40, 42, 45) and is recommended by Menander Rhetor II (438, 445–446).

In encomia to people, apostrophe is notably present at the end of the speech (Pseudo-Aristides, *Orations* 35; Menander Rhetor II, 404, 417), or in both the exordium and the peroration (Gregory Thaumaturgus, *Address of Thanksgiving to Origen* 15, 17, 204–207; Menander Rhetor II, 378, 381).

In the *Birthday Speech to Apellas* (*Orations* 30), Aristides switches constantly between the "you" and the "he." We slip progressively from the apostrophe, employed as an isolated figure, to the second person as the dominant tone of the speech. Apuleius, in the ninth piece of the *Florida*, initially addresses the audience; but arriving at the second section, which contains the encomium of the proconsul (30ff.), he no longer addresses them but turns toward the magistrate. This prolonged use of the second person is particularly frequent when the epideictic speech is not a pure encomium, but represents a step, an approach to obtain something, or an exhortation, like the welcome speech (Aristides, *Orations* 17, 21), the invitation speech (Menander Rhetor II, 424–430), or the offering of a crown (Menander Rhetor II, 422–423). The same is true for thanks: Apuleius praises Aemilianus Strabo in the third person, but addresses him directly to thank him (*Florida* 16.31–32); throughout the *Panegyric*, Pliny concurrently addresses the conscript fathers and Trajan, while still passing occasionally to the third person to praise the emperor. At times we can speak of an epideictic speech in the second person.

Encomium in the third person fixes and distances the praised object; it immobilizes it in its perfection and offers this perfect image for the audience's contemplation. It is the construction of an ethical model that the orator makes the audience admire; the *laudandus* is held aside from this demonstration, as if it did not concern him—which also allows his modesty to be spared should he attend the speech. Apostrophe to the praised object, like all figures, marks a sort of rupture: regardless of the etiquette and the established forms, it disrupts the normal allocution situation to add something to the pure encomium, either in the form of a demand or a prayer, or as feelings, like affection, gratitude, or sadness. Apostrophe is the stylistic translation of a dimension of warmth inserted into the encomiastic demonstration. This warmth is still measured when the addressee is actually present. When, on the other hand, he is absent, the apostrophe becomes paradoxical and takes on a much greater force. This explains the great pathetic force of the apostrophe to the deceased in the lamentations.

Whether categorized as a trope or as a figure of thought, hyperbole is also an audacious process.[29] It is both very important and very frequent in epideictic rhetoric. Hyperbole, by its very definition, serves to amplify or diminish:[30] in this way, it coincides with the aims traditionally assigned to praise and to blame, and is particularly suited to the epideictic genre.[31]

Rhetoricians distinguish three forms of hyperbole, one through comparison of equality, the second through comparison of superiority, and finally the pure, unreferenced exaggeration (Demetrius, *On Style* 124):

> Hyperbole . . . is of three kinds. It is expressed either in the form of likeness, for example "like the winds in speed"; or of superiority, for example "whiter than snow"; or of impossibility, for example "with her head she reached the sky." (Trans. Innes [Halliwell et al. 1995:427])

A clear illustration of these three forms can be found in an encomium of a boxer by Dio Chrysostom (*Orations* 29, entitled *Melancomas*), which indicates that the young boxer was the equal of the war heroes of Troy and the Greco-Persian Wars (14), that he was more beautiful than all of the beautiful men who had ever existed (3), and that he had been to all cities of renown and had been seen by almost all of humanity (6).

Hyperbole in encomium also appears as very frequent use of superlative adjectives and words like "only," "first," "all." Hyperbole can be applied to quantities, times, and feelings.

Before we condemn hyperbole as lies, it is useful for us to gain an appreciation of its precise stylistic worth, because the situation of this figure in relation to truth is more complex than it may initially seem. Very interesting ancient analyses, particularly Quintilian's, define the effect that hyperbole has as one of ambiguity (*The Orator's Education* 8.6.67, 73):

> [Hyperbole] is an appropriate exaggeration of the truth. It has an equal value in the opposite functions of Amplification and Attenuation. . . . But even here, a certain sense of proportion is necessary. Though every Hyperbole surpasses belief, it must not be beyond all reason; there is no surer route to *cacozelia* [bad taste]. (Trans. Russell [2001:3.465, 469])

Hyperbole is a lie, but not a lie intended to deceive. The only people to decry this as scandalous are those who follow the words to the letter; others understand that the orator is speaking figuratively and that an admissible meaning is hidden behind, or rather within, the excess. Hyperbole states the incredible, to make one believe the truth, in a sort of counter-understatement. This is the reason why hyperbole . . . must not be exaggerated! (Quintilian, quoted above). It is legitimately applied to an object which exceeds the ordinary and whose grandeur would not be sufficiently expressed in accurate words. In epideictic speech, this definition corresponds to two cases: when praising an illustrious character, for example an emperor or a famous city, and when expressing a strong emotion.

Orators consciously seek comparisons and metaphors. Let us consider, for example, comparisons to Helius (the sun). In encomia, the emperor is regularly compared to Helius.[32] Subsequently, the governor sent by the emperor is compared to a ray of sunshine, before being quickly assimilated to a star or to Helius.[33] Most certainly, these images do not claim to be original: the comparison of the sovereign to the sun, particularly, is ancient, and frequently employed in the Imperial period. But, if not new, they are very rich, because they connote radiance and glory, the idea of a model to imitate (just as the stars guide navigators), and the virtues of justice, benevolence, and providence (following the traditional conception of Helius as witness to all actions and tireless dispenser of all goods). Additionally, when applied to an emperor, the comparison with Helius is no longer merely a literary ornament and a rhetorical argument, but an allusion to the solar symbolism present in the Imperial cult. For instance, solar theology had success in the third century AD, and this situation is reflected in Menander Rhetor II's text, where comparisons with Helius are particularly insistent.

We also find series of metaphors accumulated in the same sentence, in the form of exclamations, as in Aristides' *Monody for Smyrna* (*Orations* 18.8):

> Ornament of the earth! Theater of Greece! Robe of the Nymphs and Graces! (Trans. Behr [1981–1986:2.8])

This process, as well as the many metaphors which constitute it, is borrowed directly from the poets. It appears in epideictic eloquence during the Imperial period and displays Asianist exuberance, especially adapted to lamentations. Particularly at the end of a speech or a development, the sophists like to launch a series of metaphors, which they present themselves as an effort to locate, often with the poets' help, the most appropriate designation. So Pseudo–Dio Chrysostom (Favorinus) to the Corinthians (*Orations* 37.8):

> You are now, as the saying goes, both prow and stern of Hellas, having been called prosperous and wealthy and the like by poets and gods from olden days. (Trans. Crosby [Cohoon and Crosby 1932–1951:4.35])

Or Aelius Aristides in honor of Athens (*Orations* 1.401):

> Formerly I heard with admiration, "the town hall of knowledge," and "the hearth of Greece," and "its bulwark," and all such things which were sung in praise of the city. But now all these things seem to me to fall short of the mark. If it is fitting to call a city "the lieutenant of the gods," or their "kinsman," or "the image and model of human nature," I think that

this city would have been justly so named. (Trans. Behr [1981–1986:1.77])

THE TECHNIQUE OF ENCOMIUM

The technique of encomium is noteworthy for its precision and its coherence. From the first roughing out of the plan to the different phases of composition and shaping, rhetoric has foreseen and coded practically everything. It offered a collection of lists, schemata, processes, of models, and of criteria which furnished the minds, informed perceptions, and governed social behaviors and literary creations. The encomium technique constitutes, in the strongest sense of the term, a system.

In the Greco-Roman world of the Imperial period, this system imposed itself in the same way in all the cultivated milieus and throughout the entire territory of the empire. The most different of men, in very varied circumstances and places, employed the same types of epideictic speeches, founded on the same *topoi*, the same arguments, the same plans, the same processes of composition, the same effects of style. This is why it is possible—or better yet, it is necessary—to study the texts as a series. And thus shines forth the spiritual kinship which unites the sophists practicing in Smyrna, in Antioch, and in Carthage, the consuls coming into power in Rome, the moralist preaching in Olympia or Tarsus, and also the students of the Troad and Athens, the pupil of Origen, a certain ephebe giving an encomium of the fig, or a certain philosopher composing a hermetic hymn.[34] For everyone, epideictic rhetoric served the role of a common language. The analysis of this language allows us to better understand the "horizon of expectation," which was that of all encomia in the Greco-Roman culture of the Imperial period.

Throughout this analysis, we have more often had to speak of judicious and responsible choices than of scholarly routine or of "sophistic" extravagances. We have discovered the profound importance of the topics, the pertinence and firmness of the composition through types of speeches, the variety and adaptation of the aesthetic resources—including in the most visible passages. Through all of these aspects, it is clear that ancient epideictic rhetoric was a perfectly honed technique, whose efficiency was proved in social life and which produced some beautiful literary successes.

The technique of encomium was not closed on itself. As a historical object, it was in an interdependent relationship with society's values. As an instrument of moral judgment, it stirred up questions whose responses could be found only beyond the limits of technique. These are the problems that will be explored in chapter 3.

THE CASE OF BLAME

It remains in this chapter to speak of blame, or vituperation, invective, abuse, censure, which is, in theory, the other side of encomium, but which never had the same official role.[35]

Blame is always presented, in rhetorical treatises, as the "opposite" of praise (praise is never the opposite of blame). There is a technical term for it: *psogos* in Greek, and *vituperatio* in Latin.[36]

Blame is not affected by the classifications of epideictic styles. All that rhetorical theory offers with regard to blame concerns the contents. In order to construct a speech of blame, you must start from praise, and use a formula of transposition which involves replacing virtues with vices, actions with misdemeanors, the presence or good use of exterior goods with their absence or their poor use: a formula so simple that it is often not discussed explicitly at all. For instance, Aelius Theon (*Exercises* 9[8].112) has little to say on the subject:

> These are the sources of praise, and we shall derive blame from the opposites. (Trans. Kennedy [2003:52])

Blame was regularly practiced in the field of education. The sophists of the First Sophistic particularly employed it within epideictic *antilogiai* (pairs of opposing discourses on the same topic), in line with their relativist conception of the *logos*: Gorgias, we are told, composed encomia and speeches of blame on the same subject (Cicero, *Brutus* 47). In the Hellenistic period, the blame of Penelope is cited as the object of a school exercise (Polybius 12.26b.5).

We know that the Greek and Roman schools of rhetoric during the Imperial period practiced blame in the field of preliminary exercises, even if the manuals do not always go so far as to devote a distinct chapter to it or to lengthy comment on the technique. The manuals cite as examples invectives against the brigand Eurybatus (Aelius Theon, *Exercises* 6[7].106), Philip (Aphthonius, *Preliminary Exercises* 9.28–31), Achilles, Hector, Aeschines, wealth, poverty, anger, and the grapevine (Libanius, *Progymnasmata: The Exercise in Invective* 1–8). All of these scholarly invectives are characterized by their subjects, which are drawn from ancient history and from mythology or inanimate objects. The exercise often becomes more complicated through paradox, when the invective is turned toward individuals such as Hector and Penelope, or recognized values such as richness, etc. Furthermore, perpetuating the tradition of Sophistic antilogy, the school of the Imperial period willingly inscribed its blames in antithetical compositions: for instance the *Progymnasmata* of Libanius include both an *Encomium of Achilles* and a *Blame of Achilles*, and a *Blame of Wealth* and a *Blame of Poverty*.[37]

If blame was often found in schools, its real usage appears limited. We never find blame as the autonomous object of a real epideictic speech. It was dangerous or forbidden to deliver official speeches that inveighed against the emperor, the gods, or leading citizens. Therefore rhetoric did not push the art of blaming very far. The authors who show signs of philosophy made a more vigorous and interesting use of blame. The principal example is that of Dio Chrysostom in his speeches to cities, which include reprimands or admonitions (*Orations* 31–35). In the first *Tarsic Discourse* (*Orations* 33.11) the orator himself warns the listeners:

> How much better it is to abuse people and to hold up to the light each man's stupidity and wickedness than to court favour by what is said and by compliments debauch one's auditors,

> you will discover best from what I am about to tell you. (Trans. Crosby [Cohoon and Crosby 1932–1951:3.283])

Philostratus, writing about Dio Chrysostom (*Lives of the Sophists* 487), observes that vituperation is frequent in his work; interestingly, he claims a hortative function for Dio's rebukes that is parallel to that of his encomia:

> Though he very often rebuked licentious cities, he did not show himself acrimonious or ungracious, but like one who restrains an unruly horse with the bridle rather than the whip; and when he set out to praise cities that were well governed, he did not seem to extol them, but rather to guide their attention to the fact that they would be ruined if they should change their ways. (Trans. Wright [1921:19])

Also important to recall are the pamphlets and invectives by Lucian, which are not, however, epideictic speeches in the true sense,[38] and the use of blame inserted into judicial speeches.

Therefore the global balance of blame in rhetoric seems to be showing a loss. Invectives, pamphlets, and diatribes were not absent in antiquity, not at all; but rhetorical theory of the epideictic speech of blame remained underdeveloped, and the corresponding practice scarcely ventured beyond the schoolroom. From the perspective of epideictic rhetoric, what was lacking in the speech of blame was precisely what led to the encomium's triumph: the regular recurrence, in public and private ceremonies, of a ritualized speech, with typical forms and contents, which promoted social cohesion and aimed at literary beauty. The case of blame highlights, by sheer contrast, the preponderance of the encomiastic function.

THREE

WHY EPIDEICTIC RHETORIC?

The Greco-Roman world of the Roman Empire built for itself a rhetoric suited to its new condition, and that was to a great extent epideictic rhetoric. We today may not look upon this development so sympathetically; by "we" I mean Americans, Frenchmen, and citizens of modern parliamentary democracies in general.

Accustomed as we often are to think of rhetoric on the model of Demosthenes and to require of every oration a freedom of speech worthy of the Athenian democracy (or our idea of it), we can be tempted to see in epideictic's triumph the triumph of adulation, of hollow or insincere words uttered in the context of a totalitarian regime, a useless, meaningless thing. So we must ask ourselves if epideictic rhetoric was reduced to political and self-interested flattery.

After having set forth the historical development of epideictic and established that is was a broad phenomenon, a way of functioning that affected all of society, as well as a deep and powerful technique, we find ourselves confronting another kind of problem. We must explicate the role of epideictic and understand its purpose. We must renounce our own prejudices and investigate the reason for this special taste that the Greeks and Romans had for epideictic.

TO SPEAK, SAYING NOTHING?

What, then, is it all for? To pose the question challenges an interpretative tradition solidly entrenched since Aristotle's *Rhetoric*. In defining epideictic, Aristotle indeed characterized it as a formal, ostentatious speech meant to show off the talent of the orator delivering it. In contrast to the deliberative and judicial genera, epideictic seemed to be confined to a role of gratuitous display. This conception stems from several aspects of the definition of epideictic in Aristotle's *Rhetoric*.

The symmetry established among the three genera is more apparent than real: in reality, the epideictic genus is set off from the deliberative and judicial genera, with the latter two together forming a group, that of "momentous" orations. In his introduction, and again in book 2, Aristotle totally ignores the epideictic genus, to the point that it was deemed possible that it was absent from the initial plan of *Rhetoric* and was only added as an afterthought.[1] In the examination of each genus's premises, praise is expedited much more quickly than either harangue or advocacy (*Rhetoric* 1, chap. 9).

The situation of inferiority is reflected in the list of definitions outlined above (p. 4). As for the listeners, one would expect them to pronounce on the present in the epideictic genus as they pronounce on the future in the deliberative and on the past in the judicial: the person listening to the encomium has to judge if the object of praise possesses such a virtue or quality. But Aristotle refuses this symmetry: the epideictic listener is a "spectator" or "examiner" (*theōros*) of the "ability" deployed by the orator (*peri tēs dunameōs*), while the listener in the other two genera is a "judge" (*kritēs*), deciding and settling (*Rhetoric* 1.1358b2–8); at best, he is "a sort of judge" (*Rhetoric* 2.1391b15), who has only to evaluate the quality of the speech and not to come to a decision between the antagonistic positions. This is not to say that the function of a *theōros* is not an important one, but it is different from the function of a judge.[2]

There is also a dissymmetry between the epideictic genus and the two other genera in terms of the arguments, because epideictic is thought to employ a different method from the other two; it uses amplification, which it applies to undisputed facts that merely require description, while deliberative and judicial orations, involved in debate, seek to persuade on the issues in question through examples and enthymemes (*Rhetoric* 1.1368a26–33).

Concerning form, epideictic uniquely requires a written style (*lexis graphikōtatē*), suitable for reading, whereas the other two genera have a spoken style, suitable for debate (*lexis agōnistikē*) (*Rhetoric* 3.1413b3–22, 1414a8–19).

The choice of the technical term "epideictic" (*epideiktikos*)—the very same that Plato had judged "ridiculous"—is equally fraught with consequences, because it invites identifying encomia with *epideixeis*, that is, with oratorical displays devoid of practical purpose.[3] Aristotle sees all speeches as being located in a specific situation: counsel at the assembly, advocacy at the tribunal, and encomia in the less effective *epideixeis*.

Even the order in which Aristotle numbers the genera is meaningful. In book 1, chapter 3, of *Rhetoric* the first place, given to the deliberative genus, and the last place, given to the epideictic genus, have a clear hierarchy of positioning.

To sum up, the epideictic orator recites a text meant to garner applause, whereas the adversarial orator seeks a vote through persuasion and refutation. From the point of view of immediate effectiveness, praise is in an inferior position in comparison with the other forms of oratory. It does not have a clear functionality. It is at the bottom of the hierarchy, at the top of which is found deliberative discourse, followed by judicial advocacy. Aristotle did not essentially disdain the epideictic genus, to which, on the contrary, he ascribed the highest moral aims: praising virtue and condemning vice (*Rhetoric* 1.1366a23–25).[4] But he did insist on the fact that the encomium is not involved in a concrete, present act, even as he considered it effective on another plane. That is why the system of the *Rhetoric* casts doubt on the encomium's utility and countenances defining the epideictic genus as pure spectacle.

Aristotle's notion of the "epideictic genus" was therefore a decisive step, but it was also open to questioning. Theorizing on praise as constituting the epideictic genus was dangerous in two respects: one risked treating it with contempt because its functionality within the system was unclear, and one also risked misunderstanding it because it was identified as part of an ensemble that is not coextensive, that of *epideixis*. The birth of the epideictic genus was the birth of an ambiguity that was to weigh heavily on the history of encomium.

Such ambiguity is the source of a kind of epistemological block that has prevented any in-depth thinking about epideictic's function. As a result, the moderns, victims in their turn of Aristotle's tripartite division, vied with one another in denouncing the conventional character and empty verbiage of epideictic eloquence. And thus the opinion still current today was perpetuated, according to which epideictic orations are nothing but pretty words, devoid of any practical purpose. Praise gets bad press. Unlike speeches made at the bar or before political assemblies, speeches of praise are often perceived as useless, because they lack a practical outcome. We take them to be compliments of the purest form, whose content is unimportant; or repetitive banalities; or perhaps even lies or vapid flattery.

This is why it is often said that epideictic rhetoric fulfills a purely aesthetic purpose. The audience would attend the epideictic speech as they would a concert, simply sampling the workmanship of the piece and the talent of the execution. It would be a kind of gastronomy of speeches. These analogies—to music and gastronomy—are potentially quite rich and should not be disdained. Epideictic eloquence does without doubt stir an aesthetic pleasure. Our study of its style showed the importance of the aesthetic dimension. It would be a mistake, however, to stick to just this one aspect of epideictic. To understand ancient epideictic eloquence it is necessary to reject the idle explanation of art for the sake of art, and to try to identify the aims of the speeches.

SIGNS OF DISCOMFORT WITH THE ARISTOTELIAN CONCEPT OF EPIDEICTIC

The posterity of the Aristotelian system is scattered with hints of a certain discomfort with the concept of the epideictic genus.

The separation between encomium and the two other genera, underlying Aristotle's work, was sometimes extended to the point of rendering the tripartition a bipartition. In this way, the epideictic genus is opposed to "practical" rhetoric (Gk. *praktikē*; Lat. *negotialis*),[5] or to "political" rhetoric, if we take the latter to include the deliberative and judicial genera.[6] Similarly, for Cicero and Quintilian, encomium is explicitly termed the "third genre," an expression which could relay a certain level of contempt, and which demonstrates the peripheral situation of praise in the rhetorical field.[7]

After discussions about the place of the epideictic genus within the field of rhetoric come terminological interrogations concerning the way one can define and translate the very name of the genus. This is not merely a problem of vocabulary. Behind the terminological questions lie issues regarding the definition and the function of praise.

The word *epideiktikos*, employed by Aristotle, means "delivered in an oratory exhibition." This is why Cicero and Quintilian link it back to display. So Cicero (*Orator* 37) calls it[8]

> that class to which the Greeks give the name epideictic because they were produced as show-pieces, as it were, for the pleasure they will give. (Trans. Hubbell [Hendrickson and Hubbell 1939:333])

A Latin translation that distorts the sense of this term, however, was disseminated: it is the word *demonstrativus*. Quintilian (*The Orator's Education* 3.7.12–14) writes:

> Others call it "demonstrative." . . . The latter term [sc. *epideiktikon*] however seems to me to connote display rather than

> demonstration. . . . It may be, however, that those who use the term "demonstrative" are not translating from Greek, but responding to the fact that praise and blame "demonstrate" the nature of their several subjects. (Trans. Russell [2001:2. 35–37])

The word *demonstrativus* could suggest the sense of "demonstrate," "show," "make known," "indicate" (the nature of the praised subject). In reality, *epideiktikos* usually does not mean "demonstrative" in that sense; as said above, it is rather linked to *epideixis*, "exhibition," and *epideiknusthai*, "to show oneself, to show one's talent."[9] Still worse: in modern languages, "demonstrative" conveys the idea of a logical demonstration, which corresponds neither to the Greek word nor to the Latin one.

Some people preferred to replace the word *epideiktikos* with another. The Stoics chose *enkōmiastikos*, in Latin *laudativus*, "laudatory"; this term was often adopted.[10] Such a substitution has the advantage of separating the notions of praise and exhibition, by avoiding assimilating praise and *epideixis*. But it has the disadvantage of grouping together praise and blame under one title, which only really concerns praise.

Another replacement term is *panēgurikos*, in Latin *panegyricus*, "panegyric."[11] The word *panēgyris* is used here to refer to meetings with no practical aim, which one would attend as a spectator, and is fairly parallel to *epideixis*.

Finally, there was a widening of the sense of "epideictic." Quintilian applies this word to declamations, although strictly speaking they belong to the judicial or deliberative genus, because declamation "must assume a degree of elegance" (*The Orator's Education* 2.10.12). On the basis of such usage, the wider sense of the word "epideictic" (display speech or production) is often seen in modern use, as we noted in our preface with regard to Burgess's dissertation. One can also observe advanced and heuristic ways of using the term.[12] "Epideictic" is a loose term, a fact which in itself leads us to question the identity and the destination of the "epideictic genus." The field of epideictic rhetoric seems vague and laden with poorly resolved ambiguities.

ANCIENT CRITIQUES OF EPIDEICTIC RHETORIC

Numerous critiques were made of epideictic rhetoric in antiquity. These critiques tended to involve two reproaches: that of uselessness and that of flattery.

The funeral oration (*epitaphios*)—the first preserved—made by Pericles in Thucydides already hints at an implicit denunciation of this oratory genre. From the exordium, Pericles says that the *epitaphios* is a useless and dangerous custom and that he will do it only to conform to tradition (*History of the Peloponnesian War* 2.35):

> Most of those who have spoken here in the past have commended the law-giver who added this oration to our ceremony, feeling that it is meet and right that it should be spoken at their burial over those who have fallen in war. To me, however, it would have seemed sufficient, when men have proved themselves brave by valiant acts, by act only to make manifest the honours we render them—such honours as to-day you have witnessed in connection with these funeral ceremonies solemnized by the state—and not that the valour of many men should be hazarded on one man to be believed or not according as he spoke well or ill. (Trans. Smith [1919–1923:1.319])

In the development of his speech, Pericles refuses to discuss certain *topoi*, such as the ancestors' actions, which the listeners already know, and distant ascendants (2.36). He refuses to lament (2.44). Furthermore, the orator makes much of his preoccupation with the truth (2.35, 41), and very much puts it into practice, admitting that certain deceased heroes had no doubt been scoundrels in their lifetime (2.42):

> And it seems to me that such a death as these men died gives proof enough of manly courage, whether as first revealing it or as affording its final confirmation. Aye, even in the case of those who in other ways fell short of goodness, it is but right

> that the valour with which they fought for their country should be set before all else; for they have blotted out evil with good and have bestowed a greater benefit by their service to the state than they have done harm by their private lives. (Trans. Smith [1919–1923:1.333])

Even if only implied, the criticism here is at once distinct and profound. The implication is that the traditional funeral oration is not the best way of honoring the dead, that it is made of worn-out, outdated, or pathetic developments, and that it does not shy away from lies. Rather, Pericles expounds upon the praise of the current town (2.37–41) and glorifies the military prowess of the Athenians (2.36, 42, 43). This is not a question of renouncing praise, but of conferring upon it the value of historical description and political exhortation. The orator does not repudiate the funeral oration: he reforms it, through a double movement of critique and enrichment.

So, this beautiful oration, which is often regarded as a model of epideictic speech, contains a critique against the genre. Such ambivalence is characteristic of the Greek mind. The ancient Greeks invented things and at the same time invented critical reasoning about these very things; this is true regarding the epideictic genus, as it is true for rhetoric in general, and democracy, mythology, poetry, and many other things as well. Thucydides' critique of the *epitaphios* sketches the themes that the philosophers went on to explore in more depth and ultimately to systematize.

Plato particularly critiqued praise in the *Menexenus* and the *Symposium*. In the *Menexenus*, Socrates presents his criticisms in the ironic form of a praise of praise (234c–235c). While pretending to admire the authors of funeral orations, Socrates reproaches them for being liars, because they praise the qualities their subject had as well as those he did not have. Authors of these orations make people believe these lies through the magic of their style. The power of their rhetoric works thanks only to flattery, because the listeners, likened to their ancestors, are themselves the object of the eulogy. For those making funeral orations, *eu legein* means not "saying well" but rather "speaking well of" their audience (235d). The orators' skill can be summed up in two words: lies and flattery.

In the *Symposium*, the encomia of Love give rise to an opposition between rhetorical praise and philosophical praise. Each guest makes an encomium to Love and comments on the preceding encomia; next there is the meeting between Socrates and Diotima of Mantinea (which is equivalent to a philosophical encomium to Love) and the encomium of Socrates by Alcibiades. In its prodigious richness, this dialogue, among other themes, also contains elements of a rhetorical treatise on the genre of encomium, of which all aspects are discussed. Plato criticizes futile encomia, such as the encomium of salt, and believes that only deserving subjects should be praised, like gods (177b–c, 180e). He insists upon an essential principle: one has to be able to see what the subject is, understand it, and tell the truth about it (180c–d, 185e–186a, 194e–195a); in brief, in Plato's opinion, rhetorical encomium lies, while philosophical encomium must be truthful. The technical precepts stem from this rule of truth: they include a critique of didactic and mechanical plans (as in Agatho's speech), as opposed to plans that are supple and adapted to the nature of the praised subject, and a critique of stylistic effects (195c, 198b–c, 201b), as opposed to a style that is intended to be natural and unpretentious.

Plato offers, then, a formal critique of rhetorical praise associated with a definition of philosophical praise. But the Platonic demands are such that a good encomium has little in common with what was habitually known as such. The models proposed—the encomium of Love by Diotima, the encomium of Socrates by Alcibiades—are very special compositions, which bear no resemblance to oratorical speeches and would be impossible to imitate. Rhetoric is banned in favor of philosophy.

In addition to the critiques aimed at encomium, the philosophical tradition also attacked two closely related forms: the hymn and lamentation. The usefulness of the hymn was a subject of debate in the philosophical schools. A wide range of thinkers expressed reservations regarding the encomia addressed to gods. According to many philosophers, the gods have no need for human encomia, and especially not sophistic encomia. According to Aristotle, it would be ridiculous to make an encomium of the gods, who are beyond all praise, and we must content ourselves with celebrating their beatitude: the hymn will be a "blessing" (*makarismos*), not a "praise" (*epainos*) (*Nicomachean Ethics* 1.1101b20–27):[13]

> It strikes us as absurd that the gods should be referred to our standards, and this is what praising them amounts to, since praise, as we said, involves a reference of its object to something else. But if praise belongs to what is relative, it is clear that the best things merit not praise but something greater and better: as indeed is generally recognized, since we speak of the gods as blessed and happy, and also "blessed" is the term that we apply to the most godlike men; and similarly with good things—no one praises happiness as one praises justice, but we call it "a blessing," deeming it something higher and more divine than things we praise. (Trans. Rackham [1934:59])

As for lamentation, it poses the problem of the pathetic. If passions are dangerous, all speeches that indulge in stirring them up are dangerous as well, especially those concerning sorrow, a strong passion. Furthermore, to reinforce the opinion that death and vicissitudes should be considered evil is to pervert souls. In the name of this principle, numerous philosophers condemn lamentation.[14] They say that the philosopher's duty is to console, not to lament with the afflicted. In Christianity we find the refusal to cry for the dead in the texts of certain Fathers of the Church.[15]

Latin literature contains many critiques of epideictic rhetoric. Cicero, Livy, and Tacitus mock and blame funeral orations, which contain embellishments and lies about the dead.[16] They make a Scipio of a rascal, says Varro.[17] Tacitus critiques the encomia of cities made by Greek orators. He paints a condescending image of the Greek ambassadors who present themselves to the Senate and attempt to emphasize their rights by praising their city: on the one side was the majestic power of the conscript fathers; facing them were the long-winded, vain, untruthful, and credulous orators (*Annals* 3.63):

> Deputations from other states were heard as well; till the Fathers, weary of the details, and disliking the acrimony of the discussion, empowered the consuls to investigate the titles, in search of any latent flaw, and to refer the entire question back to the senate. Their report was that . . . they were satisfied there was a genuine sanctuary of Aesculapius at Pergamum; other claimants relied on pedigrees too ancient to be clear. "For Smyrna cited an oracle of Apollo, at whose command the town had dedicated a temple to Venus Stratonicis; Tenos, a prophecy from the same source, ordering the consecration of a statue and shrine to Neptune. Sardis touched more familiar ground with a grant from the victorious Alexander; Miletus had equal confidence in King Darius. With these two, however, the divine object of adoration was Diana in the one case, Apollo in the other. The Cretans, again, were claiming for an effigy of the deified Augustus." The senate, accordingly, passed a number of resolutions, scrupulously complimentary, but still imposing a limit; and the applicants were ordered to fix the brass records actually inside the temples, both as a solemn memorial and as a warning not to lapse into secular intrigue under the cloak of religion. (Trans. Jackson [Moore and Jackson 1931:623])

The critique of encomium would continue until the end of antiquity, for instance in this account drawn from Saint Augustine's *Confessions* (6.6):

> O Lord! . . . How miserable therefore was I! And how didst thou deal with me, to make me sensible of my misery! That same day, namely, when I was preparing an oration in praise of the Emperor, wherein I was to deliver many an untruth, and to be applauded for my untruth, even by those that knew I did so. Whilst my heart panted after these cares, and boiled again with the feverishness of these consuming thoughts; walking along one of the streets of Milan, I observed a poor beggar man, half drunk I believe, very jocund and pleasant upon the matter. . . . Yea, and at that very time was there much difference betwixt him and me: for he verily was the happier man; not only for

> that he was thoroughly drenched in mirth, whenas my bowels were gripped with cares: but also for that by his wishing good luck, he had gotten good store of wine; whereas I, by a flattering oration, sought after a mere puff of pride. (Trans. Watts [Rouse 1912:1.287–291])

As for the conjunction between the critique of encomium and the critique of Greeks, a passage of Isidore of Seville's work is notable for its vigor (*Etymologies* 6.8.7):[18]

> A panegyric is an extravagant and immoderate form of discourse in praise of kings; in its composition people fawn on them with many lies. This wickedness had its origin among the Greeks, whose practised glibness in speaking has with its ease and incredible fluency stirred up many clouds of lies. (Trans. Barney et al. [1996:140])

A REFLECTION MADE BY QUINTILIAN

Few indeed were the ancient theorists who thought critically about Aristotle's definition of epideictic. The prime example is Quintilian, who notably takes issue with Aristotle to criticize the idea that the encomium could never have any other aim than ostentation (*The Orator's Education* 3.7.2–3; this important passage was quoted in full on p. 21):

> I do not deny that some themes of this kind are composed solely for display.

> But, he adds,

> Roman custom . . . has found a place for this function in practical business. (Trans. Russell [2001:2.103])

Quintilian draws attention to the idea that the notion of the epideictic genus brings together speeches which are, in reality, separated by an important difference: if some are ceremonial productions, others are in no way gratuitous and rather have a practical aim. Therefore, it would be a mistake to believe that an encomium would never fulfill anything but an ostentatious function. By way of counterexamples, he cites the encomia and invectives inserted in courtroom pleadings as well as in orations during senatorial deliberations; ultimately meant to influence the jury or the assembly, these insertions do have a practical purpose. He also cites the funeral orations delivered by holders of public office: given their official nature, these orations, according to Quintilian, cannot be reduced to mere ostentation. In short, there exist speeches of praise that are not display pieces.

These remarks point to something troubling in the way epideictic is conceived. Unfortunately, Quintilian did not elaborate on these suggestions, which could have generated fruitful reflections about the encomium's function.

THE IMPORTANCE OF EPIDEICTIC RHETORIC IN SOCIETY

In response to criticism and doubt is the simple fact that encomium was socially significant. Here is another dimension of the case to which we must now turn. The conditions of the pronunciation and publication of epideictic speeches in antiquity are proof of society's interest in this form of speech.

The speeches were made, in general, as part of ceremonies, such as religious and civic celebrations, the circumstances of political and university life, and family celebrations and journeys. In all of these situations, the speeches manifest their nature as a social act, subject to a protocol and inscribed in the process of a celebration (to which the orator sometimes alludes in the exordium or the peroration). Rarer were the cases wherein the speech was a simple reading or "reciting" which took place, external to all official proceedings, before an auditorium of listeners gathered for the event. The same speech was often made successively during a ceremony and in a public reading. For instance, Pliny the Younger read the

Panegyricus to Trajan in the Senate on the day of his coming to power, and sometime afterward he gave a long reading of the redrafted text (*Letters* 3.18).

Speeches were made in places such as theaters, council rooms (*bouleutēria*), and, in Rome, the Rostra, in the forum (where public funeral orations were made), as well as places specifically dedicated to musical and oratory performances, such as the Athenaeum of Rome and the odeons of Athens and Smyrna, the auditoriums in the basilicas and in the gymnasiums, the imperial residences, the magistrates' palaces, and, finally, private residences, which sometimes included a library and an audition room. The ancient town possessed an infrastructure remarkably suited for the practice of rhetoric, notably epideictic rhetoric—a reflection of the importance of oratorical activity in the society of the time.

The makeup of the audience for epideictic speeches was varied, ranging from a small circle of intimate acquaintances gathered for a private reading, or parents attending family events, to the mixed crowds of grand exhibitions. Whether women were present is a subject for further investigation, although they appear to have often been excluded. They had no place when the audience was composed of students, athletes, or citizens in session in the assembly. The wife of Pliny the Younger listened to her husband's lectures while hidden behind a curtain, as he himself reports; to modern ears, this account sounds as proof of hopeless male chauvinism, but in the light of ancient norms, it was intended as the self-portrait of an exceptionally attentive husband (*Letters* 4.19.3–4):[19]

> She is highly intelligent and a careful housewife, and her devotion to me is a sure indication of her virtue. In addition, this love has given her an interest in literature: she keeps copies of my works to read again and again and even learn by heart. She is so anxious when she knows that I am going to plead in court, and so happy when all is over! (She arranges to be kept informed of the sort of reception and applause I receive, and what verdict I win in the case.) If I am giving a reading she sits behind a curtain near by and greedily drinks in every word of appreciation. She has even set my verses to music and

sings them, to the accompaniment of her lyre, with no musician to teach her but the best of masters, love. (Trans. Radice [1969:1.297–299])

We do know that women attended a large exhibition by Libanius, rubbing shoulders with magistrates, the military, and artisans (Saint Basil, *Letters* 351). The wife of the deceased seems usually to be present at the funeral oration of her husband, accompanied by her children (Menander Rhetor II, 421; cf. Pseudo–Dionysius of Halicarnassus, *Rhetoric* 6.280–281). The women of the family are often mentioned in epideictic eloquence, particularly the mother and the bride,[20] to the point that we can suggest that they must have been present, at least occasionally, in the audience. The exclusion of the feminine element in the audience of the epideictic eloquence was not total.

The two points that are of most interest to the orator are the size of the audience and its quality.[21] Regarding audience size, two scenarios can be envisaged: either the orator deliberately limits the number of guests, for example when trying a new work or when reading a politically dangerous work, or the speech is truly public, in which case, the larger the audience, the more satisfied the orators show themselves to be, not only for their personal glory, but also for the impact of their words. These feelings can be translated into figures: seventeen listeners represents a ridiculous number (Aelius Aristides, *Orations* 51.34); fifty is only suitable for a private meeting (ibid. 45–46); five hundred or a thousand would be a real success (Epictetus, *Discourses* 3.23.19, 35); and we sometimes hear of several thousand listeners, which would be perfectly feasible given the capacity of ancient theaters (Dio Chrysostom, *Orations* 32.2, 20; Apuleius, *Florida* 17.18). Often among the attendants are noteworthy figures. Indeed, by its very nature the official epideictic speech is made in front of important people, notable figures of the cities, governors of the provinces, and sometimes the emperor.

During the speech, and at the end of it, the audience noisily expresses approval and disapproval. The sources establish that epideictic speeches stirred up reactions similar to those accompanying other forms of oratorical performances, lectures, and recitals of all kinds. Outbursts were welcome (Cassius Dio, *Roman History* 75.5.1):

> Severus mounted the rostra and read a eulogy of Pertinax. We shouted our approval many times in the course of his address, now praising and now lamenting Pertinax, but our shouts were loudest when he concluded. Finally, when the bier was about to be moved, we all lamented and wept together. (Trans. Cary [1914–1927:9.169–171])

Even the emperor might express enthusiasm, as Julian did when listening to Libanius' panegyric (according to the sophist in his *Autobiography, Orations* 1.129):

> I was the last to take part, for the emperor himself had so devised it that there should be the fullest possible audience, and people insisted that Hermes, in his care for his servant, stirred every member of the audience with his wand, so that no single expression of mine should pass without its share of admiration. The emperor contributed to this, first by the pleasure which he expressed at my style, then by his tendency to rise to his feet in applause, until finally when he could no longer restrain himself, despite his best efforts, he leapt up from his seat and, with outstretched arms, spread wide his cloak. Some of our boors would assert that in his excitement he forgot the dignity of his position, but anyone who is aware of what it is that makes kingship an object of reverence would maintain that he stayed within the bounds of what is proper. For what is more royal than that an emperor should be uplifted to the glory of eloquence? (Trans. Norman [1992:1.195–197])

University audiences were particularly demonstrative. At the end of recital sessions, the public could request an encore by calling for a new spontaneous speech (Aelius Aristides, *Orations* 51.40) or a supplementary session the next day (Pliny, *Letters* 3.18.4). The audience crowded around the orator, triumphantly accompanying him to his home (Lucian, *Zeuxis; or, Antiochus* 1; Philostratus, *Lives of the Sophists* 587).

All of these elements demonstrate how deeply rooted epideictic speeches were in ancient society. While discussing the way in which the speeches were pronounced, it is not inopportune to add a few words about the length of the speeches. The calculation of the lines allows us to evaluate the duration of the recitation—without forgetting that we are reasoning, by necessity, from preserved texts, which more or less reflect the speeches actually made. Following diverse estimations, and my personal tests, we can consider that the ancient orators pronounced the equivalent of eight to eighteen printed lines a minute. On this basis, the approximate results are as follows.[22] Short epideictic speeches lasted markedly less than a quarter of an hour, and the following category did not exceed twenty minutes. Encomia of emperors and panegyric speeches were made in a mere half hour. The speeches on kingship, speeches about cities, and Lucian's literary encomia generally lasted between half an hour and an hour. Dio Chrysostom's *Olympic Discourse* and Aelius Aristides' speech *Regarding Rome* lasted a little over an hour, and Gregory Thaumaturgus' *Address of Thanksgiving to Origen* lasted an hour and a half. Lastly there are interminable speeches, Pliny's *Panegyricus* (in its reworked form for the *recitatio*) and Aristides' *Panathenaic Oration*, which needed around four hours.

If we set aside these last two works, the main lesson to be learned from such calculations is the rule of measure and brevity. If we believed that the epideictic orators were incorrigible talkers, we would be very much mistaken. In fact, a normal epideictic speech lasted less than an hour, sometimes much less. To welcome a governor, to extol a god, to celebrate a birthday, a burial, or the inauguration of a building, the orator only needed ten or twenty minutes. One might dare to say that epideictic eloquence is also a study of brevity: it teaches the art of short, sharp allocution. Aelius Aristides demonstrates this in the series about Smyrna (*Orations* 17 to 21), which describes the fate of the city, struck by an earthquake, in five speeches ranging in length from less than seven to fifteen minutes.

THE SOCIAL FUNCTION OF THE EPIDEICTIC ORATOR

In the majority of texts, it is clear that the orator does not speak only for himself; instead, his words engage the different instances that either inspired the initial impulse of the speech or guided and controlled its realization or its recitation. Far from being gratuitous or arbitrary, epideictic speech would appear to be an authorized speech; its legitimacy is drawn from one or another form of mandate conferred upon the orator.

Ideally, epideictic orators are distinguished persons: distinguished as much by their wisdom and honesty as through their culture and social and political position. But these titles do not suffice, and they also draw authority from the mission conferred upon them.

The community had such an interest in rhetorical celebration that epideictic speeches were often ordered by political authorities. In Rome, the most obvious case is that of the speech of thanks by the consuls coming into power (*gratiarum actio*): this speech is organized by a *senatus consultum*, and everything spoken in it is obligatory, as are the identity of the orator, who must be one of the new consuls, and the content of the speech, which must praise and thank the emperor (Pliny, *Panegyricus* 1.2, 4.1; *Latin Panegyrics* 11.2). The official funeral oration (*laudatio funebris*) is also requested by the Senate or by the emperor, and the person making the speech must express himself in an official capacity, as a magistrate and as a relative or successor of the deceased (Appian, *Civil Wars* 2.143; Cassius Dio 44.36, 56.35).

In Greece the Athenian funeral oration (*epitaphios*) had the same official character, as the orator was elected by the assembly on the recommendation of the council (Thucydides 2.34; Lysias, *Funeral Oration* 1). During the Imperial period more than ever, a city's decisions commanded numerous epideictic types. For example, the orator who welcomed the governor, in the name of the city, through an "address" (*prosphōnēmatikos*), was elected to accomplish this task (Aelius Aristides, *Orations* 17.1; Pseudo-Dionysius of Halicarnassus, *Rhetoric* 5.273). A similar procedure was enacted for panegyric speeches (Aelius Aristides, *Orations* 46.2; Pseudo–Dionysius of Halicarnassus, *Rhetoric* 7.287).

Sometimes the speech was ordered not by the city, but by the emperor. Such was the case with the dedication speech for the Olympieion (above, p. 27). The sophists also received invitations from magistrates and influential citizens begging them to make a speech, in their homeland or abroad, on a subject of their choice.[23] The list of official speeches would doubtless become longer still if we were better informed about the circumstances of recitation of each work.

Even in the scholarly or private domain, we imagine that the orators would not take to the floor without a mandate. The partners of the educational community dictated the rules of academic eloquence. Families, who organized private ceremonies such as birthdays, marriages, and burials, trusted a person of their choosing to make a speech. Furthermore, when the subject was a notable of the city or of the empire, the boundary between private and public was erased. Ceremony spread beyond the family domain and the speech took on a public and political dimension: the family events celebrated in the Latin panegyrics are not at all private, because they directly involve the members of the Imperial family. In the words of Pseudo-Dionysius (*Rhetoric* 4.271),

> Everyone longs for this wedding. It is like a festival, a day of the new moon, a public feast of the city. (Trans. Russell and Wilson [1981:370])

The orator spoke in an official capacity, for example because he was fulfilling the role of an organizer of a sporting competition, of a priest, of an ambassador, or of the spokesperson chosen for the city, especially if he was a known sophist. Or, he was invited to pronounce the epithalamium if he was a friend of the family, for example (Menander Rhetor II, 399):

> You may . . . explain the reason why you have come forward to speak: "I am a relative of the parties to the marriage, I was in-

> vited to speak, I am returning a service for benefits received before"; or again: "I am indulging friendship," or whatever of the kind comes to mind. (Trans. Russell and Wilson [1981:135])

Again, Pseudo-Dionysius observes, regarding the speech of welcome to a governor (*Rhetoric* 5.272–273):

> There is a sort of law of principle generally observed, under which cities make a public address to these persons at their first entrance within the gates, as one might say, by the mouth of some individual chosen from those noted for their education, who speaks as it were with the public voice and makes an address on the common behalf. (Trans. Russell and Wilson [1981:371])

We can therefore conclude that epideictic speeches normally were not initiated by an individual; rather, the orator responded to an exterior solicitation, which took the form of an order, a command, or an invitation, or an institutional or legal obligation, or of a simple custom. When this solicitation came directly from the authorities, the speech had a political importance, in the strict sense; in other cases, it had more of a public or social impact, with the collective calling for and validating the speech making.

The epideictic orator is not a man who gets a group of friends together with the sole intention of demonstrating his talent: he is on a mission, and his speech is a political and social act. It is significant that this mission is often signaled in the actual speech, notably in the exordium: it is not a contingent factor, but part of the task itself. The encomiast's words have authority, which is often made more explicit by being highlighted in the speech itself. In certain cases, the epideictic orator draws his authority from his relationship with the divine. Like the poets of archaic times, he can benefit from divine inspiration, which can be seen particularly in the praise of gods (hymns) and in prayers.

We can suppose that invitations addressed to the epideictic orators were accompanied in certain cases by an offer of fees, and that encomia that pleased might be rewarded after the fact, but we have no certain information on this subject. Dio Chrysostom alludes to payment at the beginning of the *Discourse Delivered in Celaenae in Phrygia* (*Orations* 35.1):

> Gentlemen, I have come before you not to display my talents as a speaker nor because I want money from you, or expect your praise. (Trans. Crosby [Cohoon and Crosby 1932–1951:3.391])

Aelius Aristides also does this, at the end of the speech *Concerning a Remark in Passing* (*Orations* 28.153):

> I wonder that you do not notice these men who purchase their praise for money not only in oratorical displays, but also in the theaters. (Trans. Behr [1981–1986:2.139])

The money of epideictic rhetoric is discreet money (aside from games and competitions, where the prizes are published). Only the more noble forms of remuneration are envisaged *expressis verbis*, such as glory, or the possibility of making oneself known, under the cover of an official mission, and catching the attention of a governor or an emperor.

Epideictic speeches were part of a much vaster ensemble: that of praises and honors that we see awarded in all circumstances of social life, in the form of ceremonies, of portraits and statues, of inscriptions, of cheering and acclamations,[24] and of honorary decrees. Laudatory inscriptions in particular offer an important point of comparison.[25] Rhetorical encomium appears to be a part, and an important part, of the political and social system of celebration of the Imperial period.[26] The specificity of the rhetorical encomium, as opposed to other forms of homage, consists of its constructed and explicit character. In contrast to an acclamation, a monument, and even an inscription, the speech precisely details the merits, gives a global impression of the object, in the present and the past, and expresses the moral foundations of praise. The speech is a literary work and has an author; the sophist lends his reputation for intelligence and culture to the encomium.

THE PERSUASIVE CHARACTER OF THE EPIDEICTIC SPEECH

Contrary to common belief, praise consists of methodical reasoning, which aims to demonstrate. This rests on a specific notion: amplification.

We first see amplification as a technical notion in Aristotle's *Rhetoric*. Aristotle defines it as one of the forms of argumentation, alongside example and enthymeme (*Rhetoric* 1.1368a26–33):

> In general, among the classes of things common to all speeches, amplification is most at home in those that are epideictic; for these take up actions that are agreed upon, so that what remains is to clothe the actions with greatness and beauty. . . . Paradigms are best in deliberative speeches; . . . and enthymemes are best in judicial speeches. (Trans. Kennedy [1991:87])

This text sets out the fundamental distinction at the root of amplification: the distinction between the points on which there is agreement (*ta homologoumena*) and the subjects which are discussed or contested (*ta zētoumena, ta amphisbētoumena*). Whereas deliberative and judicial speeches are inscribed in a debate and try to persuade the listener on controversial questions by means of examples and enthymemes, epideictic speech, by very definition, concerns acknowledged facts, which need only be qualified.[27] Amplification is a completely specific form of argumentation. It is used to emphasize people and actions.

This combination of praise and amplification constituted a sort of dogma in rhetorical theory, reaffirmed in each period, from the *Rhetoric to Alexander* up to the authors of the end of antiquity.[28] But the concept of amplification is often misunderstood; it is necessary to discuss it in more detail to avoid misinterpretations.

First, amplification does not mean "development," even less "padding out." It involves not lengthening the speech but increasing the size of the subject, by emphasizing its importance, its beauty, its noblesse, etc. Next, we must underline that amplification is very much a form of argumentation, and not an exterior ornament. When an orator says that the agent was the first to act, for example, or compares him to other heroes, he is arguing for the quality of the object of the praise. This is the reason why, in the epideictic genus, amplification has been treated as argumentation and not as style.

The principal processes of amplification include:

• *Comparison.* Comparison is one of the best-known means of amplification, and it plays an essential role in praise. "Eulogy is best expressed through comparison" (Pliny, *Panegyricus* 53.1). It is normal to make systematic comparisons in each *topos* of the speech, and an additional, global comparison at the end. The search for illustrious and clear points of comparison is patent, for example, in the second treatise of Menander Rhetor, which compares the emperor to Romulus, to Cyrus, to the sons of Asclepius, and to Heracles (371, 375, 422); the governor, to Minos, Aeacus, and Rhadamanthus, to Demosthenes, Nestor, and Phocion (379, 380, 416); a student, to Ephor and Theopompus following Isocrates' lessons (398); a country, to Italy or Ionia (383); a city, to Athens or Rome (385, 427); a statue, to the Zeus of Olympia and to the Athena of the Acropolis (445).[29]

• *Superlative.* Attached to comparison is superlative, which supposes an implicit comparison: its use is naturally very frequent in encomium. Nothing is more common than to salute a city as "the most beautiful," a young man as "the most handsome," a governor as "the best of the magistrates." Superlatives lend themselves to stylistic effects, such as *homoeoteleuton* (identity of sound between word endings producing a sort of rhyme), *anaphora* (repetition of word in successive clauses), or *paronomasia* (wordplay depending on similarity of sound). They readily occur in twos or threes, sometimes more: a half dozen in a certain phrase by Aristides (*Orations* 23.17); ten or so in a certain paragraph by Dio Chrysostom (*Orations* 35.13).

• *Argument from uniqueness.* From superlative, we reach a supreme argument: the unique character, indicated by the word "only" (*monos, unus*). Theorists mention it at the top of the list. So Aristotle (*Rhetoric* 1.1368a10–11):

> [In epideictic] one should also use many kinds of amplification, for example if the subject [of praise] is the only one. (Trans. Kennedy [1991:85])

and Quintilian (*The Orator's Education* 3.7.16):

> What is particularly agreeable to an audience is anything that a man can be said to have been the only one . . . to have done. (Trans. Russell [2001:2.109]; modified)

• *Argument from authority.* The principle of the argument from authority consists of relying on the approval of a reputable source. The main part of Isocrates' speech in honor of Helen, for example, is built on this basis: Isocrates applies himself to listing and extolling the eminent people who have successively fallen in love with the heroine: not only Theseus, but also her suitors from Lacedaemon, Paris, the warriors of Troy, and even the gods themselves.

• *Indirect praise.* Like the argument from authority, indirect praise is also an extrinsic argument. The orator makes the merits of another object reflect back on his object. So Aristotle (*Rhetoric* 3.1418a33–37):

> In epideictic one should interweave the speech with praise, as Isocrates does; for he is always bringing in somebody [to praise]. What Gorgias used to say—that he was never at a loss for words—is similar: if he is talking about Achilles, he praises [his father] Peleus, then [his grandfather] Aeacus, then the god [Aeacus' father, Zeus]. (Trans. Kennedy [1991:275–276])[30]

• *Argument from anteriority.* This argument presumes that anything ancient merits respect. In encomium, the prestige of seniority is mentioned often, in respect to the foundation of towns and the age of gods. It focuses on a key word: "first" (*prōtos, primus*).[31]

- *Argument from totality.* Encomia like to underline the total, complete character of the power or the merits of the object: the word "all" (Gk. *pas*; Lat. *omnis, totus*, and their derivatives) is an important word in the encomiastic vocabulary—sometimes used in a hyperbolic way.

- *Quantity and quality.* Excellence is also proven through the alliance of quantity and quality. Each of these points of view, taken in isolation, is already very important. But their meeting conveys a truly complete merit. This produces the laudatory syntagms *tosoutos kai toioutos* ("so great and so good") and *kalos kai megas* ("beautiful and big"),[32] or the *puer senex* theme.[33]

Although amplification is essential to its procedures, epideictic argumentation cannot be reduced to just this technique. It is not enough to magnify the actions: sometimes it is necessary to prove that they really took place or that the praised object is really responsible for them. Quintilian illustrates this necessity in the example of Romulus, whose celestial ascendance can be praised only on condition of establishing its reality through a wide range of proofs. In addition to this positive argumentation, Quintilian continues, praise can equally require apologetic demonstrations, for example when an orator, praising Hercules, excuses his behavior with regard to Omphale (*The Orator's Education* 3.7.5–6). Similarly, the usefulness of positive demonstrations and of refutations is affirmed within praise of contemporaries (Menander Rhetor II, 368, 403, 444). All the subjects of epideictic speeches may present questionable aspects, which are no longer part of the "acknowledged points" (*homologoumena*) and which as such require proofs and reasoning in addition to amplification.

An important element in this process of demonstration is the belief, fundamental in the epideictic list of *topoi*, that actions are the manifestation of virtues. The establishment of a liaison between the acts and the person is an important form of rhetorical argumentation.[34] Here we see epideictic argumentation at work.

Moreover, there are responses to the objections.[35] The refutations of more or less widespread opinions are common currency in epideictic rhetoric. For example, in the *Agesilaus*, Xenophon responds to many criticisms leveled against the king of Sparta.[36] In the encomium of the boxer Melancomas (*Orations* 29.11, 13), Dio Chrysostom refutes the bad spirits who could say that Melancomas remained unbeaten because he died young, or that his tactic, which consisted of winning without striking blows, was not glorious. Aelius Aristides' *Panathenaic Oration* contains many apologetic passages, intended to exculpate Athens of the reproaches that had been addressed to it (*Orations* 1.34, 72, 87, 136, 154, 293), including a famous development on the questionable affairs of Melos and Scione (1.302–312). In other speeches the apology is more discreet but nevertheless present: for example when the author underlines that Imperial power, though it is shared between Marcus Aurelius and Lucius Verus, has not lost the quality peculiar to monarchic government (Aelius Aristides, *Orations* 27.30); or when he recalls that the grammarian Alexander of Cotiaeum became the preceptor of the emperors only after being recognized as the first of the Greeks and having given a thousand proofs of his talent, thereby distancing himself from any suspicion of having attained this position by intrigue (*Orations* 32.13).

The framework of Menander Rhetor's first treatise gives a large role to apology. In a general manner, this theoretician thinks that praise must include a positive part and a negative part: it is not enough to show that the subject possesses qualities, but one must prove that this subject is likewise free from defects. The orator's work includes warding off possible objections. If the epideictic orator praises a city situated up high, he will demonstrate that it is exempt, either totally or largely, from the inconveniences of altitude (cold, fog, lack of space) (351). Praising a recently founded city, he will prove that new towns are not inferior to old ones (353). If the founder has a bad reputation, he takes to his defense (355).

GLORY

Having recognized the existence of argumentation in epideictic rhetoric, it is now possible to give more depth to our study of the function of praise. If the epideictic speech uses such an arsenal of proofs, it is because persuasion is an issue.

First of all, and very important, encomia proclaim honor and glory.[37] For instance, in the funeral orations, the orators often declare that they want to bestow honor and immortal fame on the deceased through their speech.[38] So Tiberius at Augustus' death (Cassius Dio 56.41.2):

> My purpose has been that his many noble achievements should gain the meed of everlasting glory in your souls. (Trans. Cary [1914–1927:7.93])

In the ancient world, epideictic rhetoric had an honorific function. The encomium was an honor that the orator, speaking in society's name, bestowed upon the subject being praised. Praising meritorious men conferred upon them the honor owed them and accomplished what was necessary for their merits to be recognized. Delivering an epideictic speech in a ceremony was to make the contribution expected of an orator participating in a festival.[39]

The encomium was at the same time an act of justice and an obligation. It was regarded as both useful and necessary (Aelius Aristides, *To Plato: In Defense of Oratory, Orations* 3.411):

> Indeed, if someone should hypothetically remove diseases from mankind, it can be said that there would be no need of medicine, just as there is no need of a helmsman if one does not sail. But if not only all of the errors of private individuals, but also all wars should pass from mankind, oratory's affairs would not be in difficulty, nor would its power collapse, as if its roots were pulled out. For still more the national assemblies and the charms of peace require adornment from it, and so do, by Zeus, the honoring of gods and heroes and all of the laudations which are justly owed to good men. (Trans. Behr [1981–1986:1.143])

The role of spreading renown fell to orators as a moral and social duty.

THE CONNECTIONS BETWEEN PRAISE AND ADVICE

The encomia convey a message, which must be sought in the exhortation, in the advice, which draws praise closer to the deliberative genus.

Aristotle and Quintilian note that in principle there is a similarity between praise and advice: one is often advised to seek out for the future the very same qualities that are praised in those who already have them. Aristotle (*Rhetoric* 1.1367b36–1368a9):

> Praise and deliberations are part of a common species in that what one might propose in deliberation becomes encomia when the form of expression is changed. (Trans. Kennedy [1991:85])

Quintilian (*The Orator's Education* 3.7.28) tells us:

> The whole thing [*sc.* the encomiastic form of oratory] has some similarities to deliberative oratory, because its subjects of praise are often the same as the subjects of advice in that type of speech. (Trans. Russell [2001:2.117])

It is remarkable that neither Aristotle nor Quintilian draws any conclusion from this observation: they overlook the intriguing proximity between praise and advice and its contribution to the conception of praise.

Praise is often used in support of advice: the speech is principally a request, and it uses praise to make the listener yield to that request. For instance, Isocrates (*Panegyricus*) offers an encomium of Athens in order to support the city's request for hegemony; the ambassador in Menander Rhetor II (423–424) offers an encomium of the emperor and an encomium of his own city in order to support the city's request for help and allowance. Conversely, advice may appear in the extension of praise: the speech is principally an encomium, and it begins with a request or with entreaties. Such is the case of funeral orations that, after the encomium of the dead, end with consolation and exhortation to honor and imitate the deceased.[40]

The most important situation, from the point of view of epideictic rhetoric, is when praise takes on the value of advice: the speech is an encomium, with no explicit advice, and yet it contains implicit advice. This brings us to the essential point at the heart of the connections between praise and advice: the idea that praise is a piece of advice by itself. According to the prevalent understanding in antiquity, all praise—be it in verse or prose, formal or informal—possesses in itself an exhortative usefulness. It was acknowledged that praise offers listeners a model of virtue and incites them to imitate it.[41]

These indications are scattered and, let us repeat, unsystematized in rhetorical theory. From them, it emerges that antiquity represented praise as a means of moral action. On this line of reasoning, all types of epideictic perform a function of advice and exhortation. Encomia of persons provide models to admire and, if possible, to imitate; encomia of cities point out to citizens the path of virtue; hymns arouse fervor about the grandeur of the gods; encomia of marriage or festivals inspire respect for these institutions. The epideictic genus should be interpreted, therefore, as an enormous lesson whose scope must be acknowledged.

PARAENESIS AND THE VALUES BELONGING TO EPIDEICTIC SPEECHES

Epideictic deals with very diverse subjects in multiple situations. Such range leads epideictic rhetoric to set forth a vision of the world, which stretches from ethics to politics, from culture to religion. For example, rhetorical hymns express religious convictions, and epithalamia a conception of marriage and the family, even if these values are adjusted to suit the particular topic of the speech, and the circumstances and intentions of the orator. One must bear in mind here the crucial role of the *topoi* lists, which embody so many images of the world. They set forth a conception of humanity, of the city, of the divine, and, indeed, of abstractions and issues. The first lesson of epideictic oratory consists in these referential models, to which concrete situations are assimilated as much as possible and in light of which they are judged.

Epideictic orations therefore convey values about culture, politics, and religion. These values are many, and each deserves an in-depth study. Let us select two examples of important values in epideictic rhetoric of the Roman Empire. Noble birth (Gk. *eugeneia*; Lat. *genos, genus*) has a leading role, especially in encomia of individuals and cities. The first chapter in an encomium always speaks of the individuals' ethnic and familial background, of cities' founding and ancient history. Epideictic is obsessed with lineage, reflecting the structure and ideals of the society of the Imperial period, which was dominated by the influence of important families and of cities devoted to their national pasts.

"Philanthropy" (Gk. *philanthrōpia*; Lat. *humanitas*) was another core value, along with the allied ideas of benefaction and protection. Citizens and gods prized this value. Not just a mere "commonplace," it lent an overall tone to orations in some instances: for example, in hymns focused on divine benefactions or in embassy speeches that appealed to imperial munificence. By highlighting "philanthropy," epideictic reflected and enshrined an essential value in the society of the time: a value embodied in the forms of public service, munificence, and benefaction ("euergetism") in the political realm and providential intervention in the religious realm.

Thus, epideictic affirms values, and by this affirmation, its aim is to create a conviction and suggest a conduct. The encomium offers listeners models of virtue and encourages their imitation. The subject being praised inspires admiration and emulation, and listeners are meant to compete with him for the love of the good, in the hope of meriting, themselves, comparable encomia. This idea of moral example enables us to understand epideictic rhetoric's useful purpose.

That the advice rendered by epideictic orators is often obvious, and that no one would dream of arguing with it, is a common observation. When Aelius Aristides (*Orations* 25) exhorts the Rhodians, victims of a tsunami, to endure their trouble courageously and to rebuild their city, what else could they do? When Lucian (*My Native Land*) expounds upon the necessity of patriotism, who will gainsay him? When Pliny (*Panegyricus*) exhorts the emperor to be good and his subjects to respect him, when Aristides (*Panathenaic Oration*) exhorts the Greeks to revere Athens, isn't agreement a given? When the author of an epithalamium urges the young husband to perform his marital duty, wouldn't the groom be so inclined anyway? (Menander Rhetor II, 405–412: "The Bedroom Speech"). One gets the impression that the orator gives advice that his listeners already understand and follow. Are these counsels, therefore, pointless?

No, the answer is subtler. Granted that listeners already know their duty, the oration serves the useful purpose of a reminder, especially at times when hearers might be tempted to forget. Even granting that listeners always act as they should, the orations still strengthen their resolve, encourage them to persevere, and urge them to go further. Since morality can never be absolutely certain, exhortation, according to the orators, maintains a useful role, constantly renewed. So Isocrates (*Evagoras* 78–79):

> And don't think that I am criticizing you for not caring, just because I often admonish you about the same things. Both I and others have not failed to notice that you first and alone among tyrants in the midst of wealth and luxury have attempted to engage in philosophy and to labor and that you will make many kings emulate your education and desire this way of life, while abandoning that which they currently pursue. Nevertheless, although I know these things, I do and will continue to do what audiences do in athletic contests. They encourage not the runners who are lagging behind but those straining for victory. (Trans. Too [Mirhady and Too 2000:155–156])

Aelius Aristides, who remembers Isocrates (*Panegyric in Cyzicus, Orations* 27.42–43), tells his audience:

> And do not be surprised that although I have nothing to censure, I think that I should offer some advice. And do not think

> that advice is the act of only those who come to speak in criticism. But it is also the business of those who bestow praise. This is clear from that old and well-known proverb about runners. For no one, one might say, urges on those of them who are in last place and who have been completely left behind, but those who he sees are near to victory. . . . So too we now say to you nothing clever or wise, but more or less the very things which you do and in which you have been raised, that is respect for your rulers, honor for the laws, and the practice of concord, which is, indeed, a matter always to be approved, but is particularly in keeping with the present times. (Trans. Behr [1981–1986:2.106])

Some ancient rhetors and grammarians had recourse to the technical term "paraenesis" (Gk. *parainesis*) to designate the obvious counsels that no one would think of contesting (although they do not apply this term to epideictic rhetoric). These authors recognized that there are two sorts of advice: some intend to bring support in the context of a debate, in line with the traditional definition of "deliberative" eloquence, while others preach the convinced and suffer no contradiction. This duality of advice is expressed in a terminological distinction between "counsel" (*sumboulē*) and "paraenesis" (*parainesis*). The *sumboulē* is a piece of advice regarding a contested matter, while *parainesis* is an exhortation that no one can oppose at all. Unlike counsel, which aims to win approval in a debate, paraenesis is an exhortation to what is incontrovertible. "We must declare war today" is a counsel; "We must honor the gods" or "We must be wise" are paraeneses.[42] So Pseudo-Libanius (*Epistolary Styles* 5):

> Paraenesis [*parainesis*] differs from counsel [*sumboulē*]. For paraenesis is hortatory speech that does not admit of a counter-statement, for example, if someone should say that we must honor the divine. For nobody contradicts this exhortation were he not mad to begin with. But counsel is advisory speech that does admit of a counter-statement, for example, if someone should say that we must wage war, for much can be gained by

war. But someone else might counter that we should not wage war. (Trans. Malherbe [1988:69]; slightly modified)

Applying this distinction to the encomium, we may therefore conclude that, from a technical point of view, the pieces of advice given by epideictic orators belong to paraenesis. But this does not mean that all paraenesis is epideictic, as certain scholars suggest.[43] While the epideictic genus's aim is to reinforce adhesion to values, all speeches which reinforce adhesion to values are not epideictic. What is particular to the epideictic genus is that it accomplishes its paraenesis function *through the means of praise*. To forget this role of praise would lead to an excessive extension of the notion of the epideictic genus.

The idea of epideictic rhetoric as a means of advice and moral action can seem at first glance to be simultaneously edifying and passé. But in fact it serves as an excellent basis for a modern, up-to-date analysis. We are speaking of "consensus"[44] and "ideology." And what we notice, indeed, is that the principal vocation of epideictic oratory is the reinforcing of the public's adherence to accepted and recognized values. Gods, cities, sovereigns, civic leaders, institutions: it praises what everyone already respects or is thought to respect. Its purpose is not to say the truth,[45] but to reaffirm and re-create afresh the consensus around prevailing values. Epideictic rhetoric is the social order's rejuvenating bath. It instantiates a moment of communion, in which a community, or a microcommunity,[46] presents itself with a show of its own unity. Thus, the celebratory function ought to be seen in sociological terms. The encomium is the offspring of the society to which it owes its very existence, and at the same time it presents lessons in values to this society. It is not reducible to cant or flattery; it performs a social role. It delineates images and beliefs common to the group; it defines and justifies accepted values; and sometimes it grants currency to new values.

More precisely, every encomium has a double message. Even as it affirms the merits of the subject praised, it proclaims, implicitly or not, the model of excellence—contained especially in the *topoi*—against which this subject is measured. Praise of a sovereign (*basilikos logos*), for example, is not merely homage rendered to a reigning emperor and encouragement to respect the monarchy; it defines the good king. All praise devoted to a particular subject doubles as a valuable lesson for all subjects in the same category. Thus, epideictic oratory constantly operates on two levels at once: the one specific, and the other more general.

The shift to generalizing and theoretical models transforms the epideictic orator into a master of politics, ethics, theology, and so forth. The subject appears to be praised according to higher criteria. The praise bestowed is not ordinary, instinctive approbation, but the operation of elaborated and sanctioned paradigms. The orator's task is not just to strengthen listeners in their affinities and aspirations, but also to explain and justify the latter. The orator enlightens the community about its own sentiments, provides a rational foundation for its traditional practices, and translates its convictions into rhetoric's respected language.

Epideictic orators therefore shape awareness and develop a vision of the world. If other contemporary thinkers play a similar role, the uniqueness of epideictic oratory consists in seeing things from the angle of what is laudable and from the viewpoint of the community. Epideictic orators present the shining and unanimous face of the society's universal understanding. There is a "utopian" element in epideictic.[47] The encomium is a speech not totally in touch with reality, and all its richness is owing to this remove, which enables it to extol certain values. The notion of beauty reappears (see above, p. 69), but with a deeper meaning. It is a question not only of aesthetic quality but also of moral and religious worth.[48]

This function of solidifying the social order is the response we can provide to the question of the encomium's purpose. Such a perspective on epideictic rhetoric allows us to understand why it has seemed so difficult, in antiquity and still in modern times, to define the purpose of the epideictic genus exactly; for the idea of immediate effectiveness, used apropos of the other two genera, has no place here, and it was necessary to imagine a form of activity that, while no less real, was more subtle and more diffuse.

At the end of this analysis, I am still not certain I have made epideictic rhetoric beauteous to behold. But, after all, that was not my intent. We have argued that epideictic orations are not empty and hollow-sounding words, that they are not instruments of totalitarian propaganda, and that they fulfill complex functions in consolidating the social order around shared values. Certain readers will be ready to consider favorably the idea of research into consensus, while others would prefer something more subversive. I beg the latter for just a little more patience.

FOUR

NEW APPROACHES IN EPIDEICTIC

In the following pages, we would like to point out some avenues of research that are opening up today as a means to better interpret epideictic and that deserve investigation. We shall limit ourselves merely to touching upon some ideas and presenting some examples and quotations, fully aware that they demand in-depth study and hoping that they will provide material for future discussion.

ACTS OF SPEECH AND RITUALS

Epideictic, one could say, appears empty and stiff: let us take this impression as a starting point as we seek to better understand the form. It is correct that epideictic orations are rife with conventions and stereotypes. Whether he was honoring an emperor, welcoming an official, praising a city, or celebrating a god, one gets the impression that the audience knew in advance, at least in broad outline, what the orator was going to say, and so the exact content of his words had little importance. So for the time being, let's set content aside.

Granted that the specific content had little importance, the oration still draws significance from its very existence, the simple fact that a given person is delivering a given address in given circumstances. Seen in this way, epideictic oratory can be approached in light of what the philosopher of language J. L. Austin has called "performative utterances," by which he meant pronouncements that are neither instructional nor persuasive in aim but are themselves the performance of an act. For example, someone who says "Hello" is not describing what he is doing, he is doing it; he is not saying that he is making a greeting, he is, in fact, greeting. Verdicts, pledges, formulaic phrases like "I dedicate this book to you," "I thank you," "I now pronounce you man and wife," etc., are similar. These performative utterances, according to Austin, are "illocutions," that is, acts one effectuates *by saying* the appropriate words according to conventional standards.[1]

If this famous analysis were applied to epideictic oratory, each type of oration could be reduced to a performative utterance such as "I praise him," "I mourn him," "We thank you," "We acknowledge your rule," "We welcome you." . . . Linguistics teaches us that such words have a value, and that the act of saying them is in itself an act that matters, an effective homage: in short, that epideictic oratory has an aspect of "illocution."

Along with a linguistic approach, epideictic rhetoric also invites an anthropological approach because of its ritual dimension. Epideictic orations were a part of ceremonies. As speech regulated by custom, they represent an element of political, religious, familial, and/or social rituals. And that is one of the reasons epideictic rhetoric developed in late antiquity, a world where ceremony, especially courtly ceremony, was paramount.

So the utility of epideictic rhetoric resides in its performative and ceremonial worth. Here are two aspects that ancient theorists could not have imagined, because they did not have the modern tools of linguistics and anthropology at their disposal.

THE UNSPOKEN

The discourse of praise lends itself admirably to hidden meanings. The affirmation of universally recognized values is not exclusive of the adoption of more limited positions, reflecting the interests or the convictions of a group or a person. It is normal to insert precise messages in speeches of praise, in the form of not only advice, requests, and petitions but also complaints and recriminations.

For example, in the welcome speech according to Menander Rhetor II, precise demands are mixed with the ideal definition of the *laudandus*. The occasion of such a speech is the welcoming of a governor who has come to stay in the city. If the entering governor is not well known, the encomium, Menander says, should be formulated in the future tense. In broad outline the plan is as follows (377–381):[2]

Proem

The speaker shares the pleasure of the city at receiving such a good governor.

The subject population

The topic is to be treated differently according to the previous circumstances: if these were bad, "day comes after night"; if good, previous prosperity will now be surpassed. Thanks are due to the emperors.

Praise of emperors

Praises of the governor

If he has done great deeds, praise these; if not, discuss his native city or nation, or his family. On this basis, forecast his virtues: justice, courage, temperance, and wisdom.

Epilogue

Greeting of the governor as a savior by the whole population.

Apparently such a speech is a mere encomium. But behind the sweet words the listeners and the governor himself are invited to understand a request, expressed in veiled terms. Every sentence hints at the specific problems of the province, and every compliment for the future is a way of asking the governor to prove worthy of the portrait being drawn: "I am sure that [he] will be good and just to us"; "No one will dwell in prison unjustly, or be unjustly punished"; "He will represent our cause to the emperors"; etc. (379) (trans. Russell and Wilson [1981:97–99]). The congratulatory address is thus transformed into a register of grievances and a petition. The Greek epideictic orator, commissioned by his fellow citizens, uses the weapon of praise—the only weapon at his disposal—to compel recognition from the Roman authorities.

If particular aims are absorbed in the consensual function, what about critical aims? They exist, overtly or secretly, and because of them we can say that epideictic speech is not limited to expressing only acknowledged values. Notably, when the encomium is about a person who is poorly viewed by the authorities, the entire speech appears like an act of opposition: this is why Tiberius forbade the funeral oration of Germanicus in Rome (Tacitus, *Annals* 3.5), and Libanius was scared to release the funeral oration he had written in honor of his uncle and the lament on Julian.[3]

Praise in this instance is an instrument not of communion, but of dissent and denunciation.[4] In order to better understand this phenomenon, it is useful to build on the concept of "figured speech," which comes from ancient rhetoric (Gk. *eskhēmatismenos logos*; Lat. *figuratus sermo, figurata oratio*).[5] We are not talking about "stylistic figures": "figure" is taken here in the sense of "form," the shape given to an oration. The concept of "figured speech" applies to cases in which the orator uses false pretenses to disguise his real intent, or speaks obliquely in order to get to his point indirectly. The significance of this concept is not slight, when "figured speech" is revealed as a key to reading and a new means of decoding ancient works. We should remember that the ancients practiced many techniques for encryption and decryption (irony, enigma, allegory, etc.); "figured speech" is just one of these techniques, proper to the rhetorical field.

A significant case of hidden meaning in an encomium is Plato's *Menexenus* (236dff.), ostensibly a funeral oration for Athenian soldiers, but whose complex and ironic character scholars today recognize.[6] This speech shows that it is possible to play with the rules of epideictic and thereby convey messages that are within the reach of a minority of readers.

Again, Dio Chrysostom's *Discourse Delivered in Celaenae in Phrygia* comes in the form of an encomium of the city. The orator insists on the inhabitants' material prosperity: he insists so much that he arouses the reader's suspicions (*Orations* 35.14–15):

> And a very great index of your power is found in the magnitude of the contributions with which you are assessed. For, in my opinion, just as those beasts of burden are judged to be most powerful which carry the greatest loads, so also it is reasonable to suppose that those cities are the most considerable which pay the largest assessments. And what is more, the courts are in session every other year in Celaenae, and they bring together an unnumbered throng of people—litigants, jurymen, orators, princes, attendants, slaves, pimps, muleteers, hucksters, harlots and artisans. Consequently not only can those who have goods to sell obtain the highest prices, but also nothing in the city is out of work, neither the teams nor the houses nor the women. And this contributes not a little to prosperity. (Trans. Crosby [Cohoon and Crosby 1932–1951:3.405–407])

One wonders how to interpret these apparent compliments. Dio was a philosopher. Did he not mean to reproach the inhabitants for being attached to their prosperity and excessively proud of it? Praise thus turns into blame.

Some ancient texts—either philosophical or not—are quite explicit on the "figured" function of praise. The very phrase "figured encomia" (*eskhēmatismenōn enkōmiōn*) appears in the *Commentary on Plato's Alcibiades I* by the Neoplatonic philosopher Proclus (fifth century AD).[7] According to Proclus, in the *First Alcibiades*, Socrates pretends to praise Alcibiades, but in actual fact he is censuring him for his ignorance. Socrates has chosen to adopt a laudatory form of expression to make his reproach more acceptable to the young and vain man he is speaking to.

In Philostratus' *Life of Apollonius of Tyana*, the philosopher Demetrius delivers an encomium of cicadas; he next explains that his encomium serves as a way of denouncing the Imperial censorship *a contrario* (7.11):

> As they sat under a plane tree, the cicadas were singing away, softly accompanied by the breeze, and looking up at them Demetrius said, "You blessed, truly wise creatures, it seems the

> Muses taught you a song not subject to lawsuits or accusations. They made you superior to greed, and settled you far away from human envy in these trees here, where you blissfully sing of your happiness and the Muses." . . .
>
> "I did not mean this as an encomium," said Demetrius, "but as an illustration of the fact that these are permitted their own concert halls, but we are not allowed to make a sound, since wisdom has been turned into an offense." (Trans. Jones [2005: 2.227–229])

Pliny the Younger describes another scenario: if an orator praises someone for nonexistent qualities, the *laudandus* may regard the encomium not as naive flattery, but as disguised reproach. That would happen under Domitian, Pliny says. But of course there is no danger of that happening under Trajan, since *he* is a good emperor and deserves the praises that are awarded to him (*Panegyricus* 3.4). This quotation from Pliny is interesting because it gives voice to the possibility of double interpretation:

> There is no danger that in my references to his humanity he will see a reproach for arrogance; that he will suppose I mean extravagance by modest expenditure, and cruelty by forbearance; that I think him covetous and capricious when I call him generous and kind, profligate and idle instead of self-controlled and active, or that I judge him a coward when I speak of him as a brave man. (Trans. Radice [1969:2.329])

If we continue in this manner, we see that it is possible to uncover in Greek epideictic masterpieces of the second century AD certain discreet and calculated departures from the encomium's official norm. On the question of the relations between Greek-speaking elites and the Roman government, a delicate issue, epideictic rhetoric provided stealthy forms of expression and shifty discourse, in which hidden doubts and disagreement could find voice in the most apparently enthusiastic adulation. Let us cite a few examples from Aelius Aristides' works.[8]

Both by its structure and by its style, the speech *Regarding Rome* (*Orations* 26)—Aristides' masterpiece—follows the rules of rhetorical praise. The orator starts by emphasizing the difficulty of the subject, then describes the merits of the situation of Rome, then glorifies at length the civil and military organization of the Roman Empire, before finishing with a brilliant synthetic tableau:

Proem. Difficulty of the subject (1–5)
Geographical situation (6–13)
Civil policy and administration. Comparison with other empires (14–71)
Military policy (72–89)
Constitution (90–91)
Synthetic tableau. The empire flourishes in peace (92–106)
The emperor (107)
Peroration (108–109)

The presentation is conducted with a large number of comparisons, and with an admiring and hyperbolic tone. Up to this point, all is normal and expected, following the norms of encomium. But the speech is interesting because of what it does not say.

In more than thirty pages, representing approximately one hour of speaking, Aristides finds a way to say nothing about the origins of the city, nor the supposed relations shared between the Greeks and the Romans, nor the stories surrounding the founding of Rome. He says nothing about the history of Rome. He completely neglects its monuments, architecture, art, literature, and language. He says not one word about Romulus, the Scipios, Caesar, or Augustus. The only celebrated Roman he refers to is Aeneas, through an allusion to Homer (106). He does not mention a single Roman proper name, nor does he speak a word of Latin.

In addition, there is a second series of notable omissions in this discourse: they concern the Roman conquest. Aristides avoids saying that the Roman Empire was forced upon the Greeks. At the very most he allows himself to allude to the traditional play on the word *rhōmē*, which means both "Rome" and "force" (8). But he does not develop this idea. He says nothing about the military and political processes that led to the installation of Roman domination over the Greek world.

How should one interpret these omissions? It would have been advisable to mention these points in an encomium of Rome, since they are part of the *topoi* of praise of cities. Consequently, one has to reckon with a series of deliberate choices. Aristides wanted to portray Rome only as the imperial capital, the city from which domination over the provinces was exerted. He chose to treat only the current state of affairs, the existing functioning of the empire in the political domain, which allowed him to avoid mentions of the local color, as well as all of the artistic, religious, mythological, and historical facts concerning Rome (Greek mythology and history are abundantly referred to).

Here we have an example of eloquent silence, a device attested in the rhetoric of "figured speech." The theoreticians consider a case in which the orator is confronted with a weighty and well-known situation, about which he does not have the right to speak and to which he can refer only implicitly.[9] In the case of *Regarding Rome*, the secret that everybody knew about was the domination that the Romans imposed on the Greeks. This heavy truth weighed on the speech, but Aristides could not allow himself to speak about it openly. He therefore proceeded by omission, an omission so drastic that it became significant in itself and served as the carrier of a hidden message.

Therefore, this speech is much less flattering than one might have previously thought, and it incorporates a certain audacity. Aristides suggests that the Roman Empire is a system imposed on the Greeks from the outside, and that the Greeks submitted to their rule without feeling any admiration for Roman civilization and culture. Such is, we can believe, the encrypted message of *To Rome*, which is a deeply realistic and embittered message, if one knows how to read between the lines. Aristides weights his praise and concentrates on what he approves of, namely the material benefits of Roman peace. As for the rest, he makes himself understood without having to spell it out, by intimating that Roman culture does not matter, and that Roman domination must be endured with resignation.

In certain cases, it is in the details of the text that one must seek discreet hesitation or veiled reproach. We can now turn to the examination of some scattered passages that express the same disenchanted attitude toward the Roman Empire. The process of "figured speech" that is implemented here could be called the "hidden key": a variant of the general method that consists of saying one thing while suggesting something completely different. It involves slipping a parenthetical remark into a discourse that casts the whole argument in new light. This process is analyzed by Pseudo–Dionysius of Halicarnassus, who perceived the model of it in texts by Homer and Plato. The orators who use this process, according to Pseudo-Dionysius, begin by developing at length an opinion that the audience already agrees with, then throwing out "as an afterthought," "at the end," an additional point, which is the one that the orator truly believes (*Rhetoric* 9.6):

> What is this art? It is, after having spoken on a subject that carried conviction, to introduce at the end, incidentally, the most pertinent subject. (My translation)

I would like to draw attention to two passages that fit this definition.

In *The Panathenaic Oration* (*Orations* 1), Aelius Aristides sings the praises of Athens. He looks over the history of the city, from mythological times to the Battle of Chaeronea (338 BC), which established the domination of Macedonia over Greece. Here he stops, due to a lack of time—or so he says—and in this passage he slips in two sentences about the present situation. Aristides acknowledges that the situation of Athens has changed, and he makes it clear that this new situation is a product of the Roman Empire. Following a method that we are starting to recognize, Aristides expresses no criticism. On the contrary, he extols the happiness of Athens under the power of the Roman Empire, and he displays his own loyalty by expressing the wish, twice, that this power would last forever.

He then goes on to state (*Panathenaic Oration* 332, 335):

> The present empire of both land and sea—and may it be immortal—is not unwilling to adorn Athens as a teacher and foster father, but so great are its honors that now the only difference in the city's condition is that it is not involved in troublesome affairs. But for the rest, it is almost as fortunate as in those times, when it held the empire of Greece, in respect to revenues, precedence, and the privileges conceded by all. . . . Under the one [*sc.* empire] at present existing, which is in every way the best and greatest, [Athens] has precedence over all the Greek race, and has fared in such a way that no one would readily wish for its old state instead of its present one. (Trans. Behr [1981–1986:1.67, 68])

Athens is happy under Roman domination because it is free of the political and military responsibilities that it assumed before, and it enjoys honors and supremacy among the Greeks. In sum, the city has been rid of inconveniences and only the advantages remain. Is everything better then? Athens is today "almost" (*mikrou dein*) as happy as it was in the past, and one would not "readily" (*rhaidiōs*) wish for it to return to its former state. If one gives these words their full weight, they betray a reserve and throw doubt on the overt encomium of Rome.

Out of one hundred pages of mythological and historical statement, these remarks occupy a total of ten lines, yet they beg the essential question of the situation of Athens in the Roman Empire (and, through Athens, the situation of all Greeks), and they suggest that the evaluation of this situation is not simple. This is the burning question, the heart of the problem. For precisely this reason, Aristides did not want to keep silent on the subject, but he did not want to address it head-on. He deemed that it would be cleverer and more prudent to resort to a process of "figured speech" by slipping into his text, fleetingly, words that had great resonance. This "almost" is a nugget, and it was up to his audience and readers to discover it and to draw conclusions from it for themselves.

In *Oration* 2, which develops a long refutation of Plato's charges against rhetoric, the assessment is identical to that of the *Panathenaic Oration* (Aristides, *To Plato: In Defense of Oratory* 430):

> If someone should be of such a nature so that he does not easily appear before the people with his oratory and engage in political disputes, since he sees that the government is now differently constituted. . . . (Trans. Behr [1981–1986:1.146])

We have to wait until paragraph 430 of the discourse to come across this remark, thrown in as if an afterthought but in reality of great importance. It signifies that the situation changed between the time of Plato and that of Aristides because the Greeks were, from then on, under the Roman Empire. Leaving for a moment the Platonic problem, Aristides finally refers to current events. He acknowledges the political situation and recognizes that this change has an impact on rhetoric, insofar as the Greek orators of the Roman era, contrary to their predecessors of the Classical era, no longer have the capacity to treat the important issues that engage their existences and the functioning of the states.

The present remark invites the reader to examine the changes that occurred during the Imperial era. This would be the subject matter of a long discourse. Aristides was fully aware of the pertinence of this topic, and he was keen on addressing it, but in his own way: he suggests the importance of it through a remark made implicitly in one sentence. This strategy was clear to those who knew to listen for it.

It would be useful to reread the corpus of epideictic rhetoric following this method, with the possibility in mind that the orators are suggesting more than they say outright and that there are innuendos and things left unsaid. This is a vast undertaking, requiring enormous care, but would lead to a new view of epideictic. It would allow us to discern hidden messages, idiosyncratic positions (reflecting the interests or convictions of a group or an individual), and sometimes even veiled criticisms behind epideictic orations' universally approving and sanctioning tone.

THE PSYCHOPATHOLOGY OF THE ENCOMIUM

The notion of "message" leads us to a further topic, the encomium's listeners. Aristotle notes this problem, without developing it (*Rhetoric* 1.1367b7):

> Consider also the audience before whom the praise [is spoken]. (Trans. Kennedy [1991:83])

In principle, the encomium produces pleasure in the audience. By definition, it is full of elevated sentiments, glorious deeds, magical sites, and kindly gods. It transports listeners into a rarefied realm where beauty reigns in all its forms. Epideictic is not only a feast of words, but also a feast of moral, aesthetic, and religious sense. Listeners are thought to draw pleasure from all these beauties. There is a reason for optimism in learning that the new governor is an upright and experienced administrator. There is a certain satisfaction in assimilating fresh details of the lives of leading men or the emperor's most recent military campaign, and in discovering thus, once again, that the leaders of society are virtuous and the empire well ruled. And even if all this is already known, what pride, what reassurance to experience, for example, the commemoration of one's own city's greatness, or the providence of the gods whom one adores! This is what the encomium is primarily: a communion in the ritual of merit, a moment of shared bliss.

Less peaceful feelings, however, trouble this kingdom of bliss and joy. First of all, an epideictic speech may be boring or inopportune. Let us cite an amusing instance from the last chapter of the thirteenth-century historian George Akropolites' *History* (89):

> I had written an oration on the subject of the deliverance of the city of Constantine. The theme of the oration at the beginning was thanksgiving to God for His beneficence to the Romans and His compassionate solicitude and help, but there was mixed with the oration also a panegyric expressing thanks to the emperor. The request at the end of the oration was for the emperor's first-born son, Andronikos Komnenos, to be pro-

> claimed together with the emperor his father. This was unknown to most people, especially those in office who did not approve of the matter. Our leading men, the despot John, the emperor's brother, and his father-in-law, the sebastokrator Tornikes . . . , not knowing the theme of the oration and the request for the promotion, pressed the emperor to hear the oration. The emperor was annoyed, for already the sun was casting its midday rays and the time for the midday meal was passing . . . (Trans. Macrides [2007:386–387])

We shall never know the end of this curious and complex story, since the text breaks off in midsentence. It sounds as if the emperor had to listen through the entirety of the speech and postpone his lunch.

Concerning the audience, it is often emphasized that the encomium risks provoking their "envy" (Gk. *phthonos*; Lat. *invidia*) of the subject being praised.[10] This reaction can be avoided only when the listeners recognize the *laudandus*'s overwhelming superiority but even in that case the orators must take a lot of precautions. So Aelius Aristides praises Athens (*Panathenaic Oration* 402):

> Therefore, O men of Greece, it is reasonable that you neither are envious of the city nor feel shame in giving precedence to it, but that you aid in its increase as far as you can and feel pride therein. For when the Athenians prevail, the victory is yours. It would be impossible for all men to be the best of mankind. But just as whenever a general is superior, his city shares in his glory, so when the leading city is properly honored, all men participate in its sense of pride. (Trans. Behr [1981–1986:1.77])

And Tiberius praises Augustus (Cassius Dio, *Roman History* 56.35.5–6):

> For who does not realize that not all mankind assembled together could worthily sound his praises, and that you all of your own free will yield to him his triumphs, feeling no envy at the thought that not one of you could equal him, but rather

> rejoicing in the very fact of his surpassing greatness? For the greater he appears in comparison with you, the greater will seem the benefits which you have enjoyed, so that rancour will not be engendered in you because of your inferiority to him, but rather pride because of the blessings you have received at his hands. (Trans. Cary [1914–1927:7.79])

As for the encomium's beneficiary, his mind swells and burgeons with arrogance, the result of vanity (Dio Chrysostom, *On Kingship*, *Orations* 4.128):

> So it is with the ambitious: When good repute and praise come their way, their souls are magnified and swell and show a wondrous burgeoning, just like the shoot of the sacred olive that they tell of at Athens, which swelled and grew to full size in a single day. (Trans. Cohoon [Cohoon and Crosby 1932–1951:1.227–229])

As Plato wrote ironically, it is not difficult to praise the Athenians to the Athenians (*Menexenus* 235d, 236a). Aristotle cites this affirmation of Socrates, but he does it with a different meaning: not to discredit praise as a flattery but, on the contrary, to underline the difficulty of praising well and in an appropriate manner (*Rhetoric* 3.1415b28–32):

> In epideictic, . . . one should make the hearer think he shares the praise, either himself or his family or his way of life or at least something of the sort; for what Socrates says in the funeral oration is true, that it is not difficult to praise Athenians in Athens, but among the Spartans [is another matter]. (Trans. Kennedy [1991:264])[11]

Or, on the contrary, the beneficiary might become anxious, worried as much by excessive as by inadequate praise. As Dio Chrysostom says in the passage quoted above, the ambitious cannot endure blame (*On Kingship*, *Orations* 4.128):

> But, alas! They soon wither again and droop and die when censure and obloquy overtake them. (Trans. Cohoon [Cohoon and Crosby 1932–1951:1.229])

But excessive praise is also a source of difficulty. Thus Iolaus implores Demophon (Euripides, *Children of Heracles* 202–204):

> I have said enough to the city: for indeed to praise too much is hateful, and I myself know that I have felt disgust at being overpraised. (Trans. Kovacs [1995:31])

And Clytemnestra implores Achilles (Euripides, *Iphigenia at Aulis* 977–980):

> Ah, ah! How can my words avoid praising you excessively? How can I avoid falling short and losing your favor? For when the good are praised, in some fashion they hate their praisers if they praise to excess. (Trans. Kovacs [2002:275])

Some people blush even when receiving legitimate praise, out of sheer modesty.[12] The orator in the act of praising always gives the impression either of saying too much, or not enough, or of glossing over some suggested digressions. There thus exists not only a psychology of the encomium, but a psychopathology, in which the pleasure felt becomes unhealthy or turns into pain the minute vanity, flattery, or suspicion starts to corrupt the relation between praise and merit.

Self-praise is yet another form of pathology.[13]

On these interesting problems, we can cite two sharp analyses, one ancient and the other modern, which magnificently describe the complexity of the matter and go so far as to speak of "hatred" and "disgust." The first is in Lucian (*How to Write History* 11–12):

> I need not say that eulogies may be pleasing to one man, him who is praised, and annoying to others, especially if they contain monstrous overstatements, the kind that most people make when they seek favour from those who are praised, per-

sisting until they have made their flattery obvious to everyone. They do not know how to do it with any skill nor do they cover up their obsequiousness; no, they rush at it, laying it all on thick, so implausible and so naïve. So they do not get what they want most: those they praise hate them the more and turn their backs on them as toadies, and rightly so, especially if they are manly in spirit. (Trans. Kilburn [Harmon, Kilburn, and Macleod 1913–1967:6.17–19])

A modern analysis was put forth by Nietzsche (*The Dawn of Day* 4.273):

> Praise. You see someone who wants to praise you. You bite your lips; your heart shrivels. O, that this cup might pass from you! But it does not pass; it comes near! Let us drink in, then, the sweet impertinence of the payer of compliments, let us transcend the disgust and deep disdain the essence of his praise inspires within us, let us put on a happy face dimpled with gratitude! He wanted to be nice to us! And now that that's over, we know how exalted he feels, he has vanquished us—and himself too, the cur!—since it was not easy for him to wring these praises from himself. (Trans. W. E. Higgins)

RELIGIOUS EPIDEICTIC RHETORIC

A tale in Philo of Alexandria underlines the importance of religious epideictic rhetoric (*Noah's Work as a Planter* 127–131):

> When, they say, the Creator had finished the whole world, He inquired of one of His subordinates whether he missed as having failed to be created aught of created things beneath the earth or beneath the water, aught found in air's high realm or heaven's, furthest of all realms that are. He, it is said, made answer that all were perfect and complete in all their parts, and that he was looking for one thing only, namely the word to sound their praises, which should make the surpassing ex-

> cellence that marked even the most minute and inconspicuous among them the subject of announcement rather than of praise, seeing that the mere recounting of the works of God was in itself their all-sufficient praise, for they needed the embellishment of no extraneous additions, but possessed in the reality that could not lie their most perfect encomium. The story runs that the Author of the universe on hearing this commended what had been said, and that it was not long before there appeared the new birth, the family of the Muses and hymnody, sprung from the womb of one of His powers, even virgin Memory, whose name most people slightly change and call her "Mnemosyne." . . . Having learned, then, that, in all that has to do with shewing honour to God, one work only is incumbent upon us, namely, thanksgiving, let us always and everywhere make this our study, using voice and skilful pen. Let us never tire of composing eulogies in prose and poetry, to the end that, whether with or without musical accompaniment whichever of its appointed functions the voice may exercise, be it eloquent speech or song, high honour may be given both to the world and to the Creator of the world. (Trans. Colson and Whitaker [1929–1943:3.277–279])

Praise of the gods and divine creations, to which Philo here invites all men—veracious praise, and limited to facts—poses the problem of religious epideictic rhetoric and rhetorical hymns.[14] Religious epideictic rhetoric displays strikingly specific features compared to other forms of epideictic. Its subjects are unique, transcending limitation and human aims, since it deals with gods and the divine. Unique as well is the orator's role, because the religious orator is an intercessor between gods and men, a "holy man" (*theios anēr*), endowed with efficacious speech akin to magic or the sacramental.[15]

The link between rhetoric and religion is, in a certain sense, obvious. Religion is intimately linked with words. The spoken and written word plays an essential role in religion, as language is necessarily used in a relationship with the divine and the sacred that includes the different forms of expression addressed to God, the different ways of speaking about the gods or about God, and the expression of religious feeling or awareness. All these phenomena can be regrouped within the term "rhetoric," covering both forms of expression in the broad sense of the word, and the art of discourse, in the strict sense, as it was codified, taught, practiced, and discussed throughout history.

We should not forget, however, that for many people, linking rhetoric and religion remains something new and daring. When one says that religious discourse can be seen rhetorically, as a persuasive speech following set forms and structures, he or she arouses suspicion. The scholars who make investigations in this direction may be suspected of adopting a rationalist attitude and of misunderstanding the very basis of religion, that is to say, belief, the notion of the transcendental. And if they apply the rhetorical approach to Christian texts, to the Scriptures, or to the Fathers of the Church, they may be accused of being subversive, on the grounds that in emphasizing rhetoric, they run the risk of undermining our understanding of faith and of theological doctrine. Many academic circles remain, even today, reticent and unenthusiastic when it comes to a rhetorical reading of ancient religious texts, whether they be pagan or Christian.

Therefore it is still unavoidable to emphasize the usefulness of the rhetorical approach in the field of religion.

Hymn (defined, in the ancient sense of the word, as an encomium to a god, accompanied by an invocation and an address) offers an example of the connection between epideictic rhetoric and religion. There is a type of rhetoric in hymn. Furthermore, there are links in this area to be established between paganism and Christianity, insofar as the same forms of epideictic were utilized in pagan and Christian contexts.[16]

The example of hymn leads us to suggest that there was, in the first centuries of the Roman Empire, a rhetorical language of religious experience that was common to both pagan and Christian communities. After all, this is not altogether surprising, as pagans and Christians lived in the same world and used the same languages (Greek and Latin), even if they held different traditions and faiths; Luke and Paul were partly Hellenic in culture. What is interesting is to go beyond this general observation, to try to establish the list of essential elements that constitute this common rhetorical language. *Topoi*, argumentation, stylistic devices, and phraseology are part of it.

This observation now raises a question: is it not the case that the similarities we can note occur on a very general level? Could we not find the same language in other places, at other periods in time? For example before—in the Old Testament—or indeed afterward—in the age of the Fathers of the Church, when the problem of the fusion of Christianity and pagan culture was very explicitly stated—not to mention in other civilizations? The question that arises is whether all in all there are universal aspects of religious rhetoric, anthropological and psycholinguistic constants, or at least essential and invariable rules. This would include, for example, in the case of encomium addressed to a god, praise of his acts, praise of divine power, and thanksgiving.[17]

The epideictic questioning allows us to go beyond the differences between particular religions and to identify fundamental rhetorical forms, so that a new angle can be brought to the study of religion.

COMPARATIVE EPIDEICTIC RHETORIC

Comparative rhetoric is a relatively recent methodology.[18] It consists of juxtaposing the forms of discourse used in civilizations different from one another and separated in time and space, so as to recognize their differences but also their sometimes startling resemblances.

Epideictic lends itself to this comparative approach, because it responds to widely found rituals: laments over the dead, epithalamia in honor of marriage, welcoming speeches greeting an important person, etc.

As we noted above with respect to hymns, one may wonder, in certain cases, if one is not in the presence of true *invariables* of epideictic, that is, of encomiastic methodologies that have universal, or at least very broad, application. This question arises, for example, apropos of some "commonplaces" of the encomium (birth, upbringing, deeds), some aspects of the associative method (joining encomium and lament in the funeral oration), some types of argument ("the first," "the only," etc.).

In fact, one finds epideictic everywhere and in every age. In Europe, it flourished in antiquity and in Byzantium, but also, for example, in Renaissance Italy, in France of the Ancien Régime, and in numerous modern states.[19] Even today, all around us, despite the disappearance of formal, classical oratory, there are many occasions, great and small, where epideictic eloquence is still employed, whether in academic or university settings, in the activities of social, religious, or political life, in all sorts of ceremonies, and even in the informal preliminary speeches (corresponding to the Greek *prolaliai*) that we still use to introduce ourselves or to introduce conference speakers. A former president of the International Society for the History of Rhetoric, the late Carl Joachim Classen, provided this telling example: a work in German called *Der Bürgermeister spricht* (The mayor speaks), published in Munich in 1953, which contains model speeches for weddings (long and short versions), for the opening of a cemetery or a swimming pool, for a fireman's funeral, and so on. This is precisely the modern version of Menander Rhetor's second treatise![20]

Additionally, one encounters in cultures far removed from our own forms and conceptions comparable to those of ancient epideictic. For example, the journal *Rhetorica* has taken note of literary laments in ancient Egypt, criticism of deceitful speech in Taoism, and an Aztec collection of ceremonial and paraenetic addresses.[21] African bards "recount or sing the glorious deeds of warriors and kings, of famous holy men or of those who offer hymns to the gods of the Bambaras."[22] The epideictic enterprise is an anthropological phenomenon found—with important distinctions, naturally—in many human societies.

EPILOGUE

Epideictic gradually earned its place within the field of rhetoric, and following its irresistible rise it triumphed in the Greco-Roman world of the Imperial age. At this high point, epideictic technique was much more than a repertory of procedures. It set forth structures, an aesthetic, and a system of representations. It was an abstract tool that permitted recognition and expression of society's values.

For us today, the Greco-Roman evidence is valued as our intellectual heritage, at least in the North American and European world, where the ancient tradition has exerted a direct and major influence. It has paradigmatic value because, leaving questions of origin aside, the Greco-Roman material stands as a remarkably full and developed corpus, despite the losses it has incurred. We find within this body of writing both theory and practice, elementary textbooks beside great works of literature, a triumph of epideictic oratory itself, and critical reflection upon it. Studying ancient epideictic rhetoric brings to light a grammar of praise and reveals ceremonial oratory's social and ideological purpose. The ancient world was an epideictic laboratory: there is much to be learned from the formulas tested there.

NOTES

CHAPTER I: THE UNSTOPPABLE RISE OF EPIDEICTIC

1. Loraux 1986; Prinz 1997.

2. It is well known that recent decades have seen a revaluation of the rhetoric of the sophists: see for instance Cassin 1995; Consigny 2001; Giombini 2012; Jarratt 1991; Poulakos 1995; Romilly 1975, 1992; Valiavitcharska 2006.

3. Radermacher 1951:130–131. On paradoxical encomium, see Pease 1926; Dandrey 1997; Peri 2001–2002.

4. Walker 2011:119–120.

5. Demont 1993; Jouanna 2012.

6. These speeches are characterized by the verb *epideiknunai* or the noun *epideixis*: Plato, *Protagoras* 328d; Philostratus, *Lives of the Sophists* 482–483 (see the apologue of Prodicus in Xenophon, *Memorabilia* 2.1.21ff.); Isocrates, *Encomium of Helen* 15.

7. However, we shall note further that the status of the epideictic genus is less clear than this table suggests; see chapter 3.

8. Pernot 2011b.

9. On the classification of the genera, see Chase 1961; Garver 2009; Hinks 1936; Mirhady 1994; Pepe 2013.

10. Rufus, *Rhetoric* 2 (Patillon 2001b:276); Syrianus, *Scholia to Hermogenes* (Rabe 1892–1893:2.11); Nicolaus, *Preliminary Exercises* 8.55.

11. Pernot 1993b.

12. In a humorous vein, see Sterne, *The Life and Opinions of Tristram Shandy*, vol. 2, chap. 17: "How the duce Corporal *Trim*, who knew not so much as an acute angle from an obtuse one, came to hit it so exactly; — or whether it was chance or nature, or good sense or imitation, &c., shall be

commented upon in that part of the cyclopædia of arts and sciences, where the instrumental parts of the eloquence of the senate, the pulpit, and the bar, the coffee-house, the bed-chamber, and fire-side, fall under consideration."

13. *Papiri della Università degli studi di Milano (P. Mil. Vogliano)* 3.123: see Cazzaniga and Vandoni 1957.

14. Grandjean 1975; Robert 1971, 1977.

15. Durry 1942; Kierdorf 1980.

16. Lévy 2001; Smith and Covino 2010; Romeo 2012.

17. For a general survey see Whitmarsh 2005; Johnson and Richter (forthcoming).

18. On education and the *progymnasmata* see Clark 1957; Cribiore 2001; Kennedy 2003; Vix 2010.

19. See Maehler 2002; Pordomingo 2007.

20. *Inscriptiones Graecae* II^2 2024 (line 134); 2087; 2115 (lines 27, 46); 2119 (I, lines 177, 189; II, lines 131, 147, 201; III, line 164). See Follet 1976:318–328.

21. Two treatises are preserved under the name of Menander Rhetor, but they are from two different authors and it is impossible to determine with certainty which one is the true Menander. The convention (followed in this book) is for the authors to be designated Menander Rhetor I and Menander Rhetor II.

22. Gangloff 2009; Goeken 2012; Pernot 2007; Velardi 1991.

23. On contests see Robert 1970, 1982:228–229, 1984.

24. Meritt 1931:19.

25. Wörrle 1988.

26. Miranda De Martino 2007:210; Di Nanni Durante 2007–2008:13.

27. See Robert 1938.

28. For the figures see Pernot 1993a:91–92; same conclusion in Manieri 2010–2011:674. On the problem of prizes see also Le Guen 2010.

29. These precedents are notably studied in Cairns 2007.

30. On epideictic and poetry see Walker 2000. On encomiastic poetry (in various periods of antiquity) see, e.g., Barbantani 2001; Bowie 1989a, 1989b, 1990, 2002; Davies and Pomeroy 2012; Esteve Forriol 1962; Furley 1995; Furley and Bremer 2001; Garzya 1983:83ff.; Guipponi-Gineste 2010; Hardie 1983; Hunter 2003; La Bua 1999; Miguélez Cavero 2008:340ff.; Nagy 1979, 1986; Norden 1899; Race 1987; Romeo 2004; Schindler 2009; Viljamaa 1968.

31. On "entries" see Bérenger and Perrin-Saminadayar 2009; Dufraigne 1994; Ernst 2012; Halfmann 1986:112ff.; MacCormack 1972; Pont 2009.

32. *Odyssey* 13.38–46 (cited by Menander Rhetor II, 430); Sophocles, *Ajax* 815ff.; Euripides, *Alcestis* 280ff.; *Children of Heracles* 574ff.

33. Aelius Theon, *Exercises* 8(10).115; Hermogenes, *Preliminary Exercises* 9.20 (trans. Kennedy [2003:47, 85]).

34. Discussion in Pernot 1993a:61–62.

35. E.g., Dio Chrysostom, *Orations* 28–29; Aelius Aristides, *Orations* 31–32; Pseudo-Dionysius of Halicarnassus, chap. 6; Menander Rhetor II, 418–422.

36. On consolation and lament see Alexiou 2002; Alonso del Real 2001; Baltussen 2013; Favez 1937; Fowler 1987; Holst-Warhaft 1992; Johann 1968; Kassel 1958; Martino 1958; Ochs 1993; Soffel 1974.

37. See Horstmann 2004; Russell 1979.

38. See for example, Fronto, *Correspondence*: *Ad M. Caesarem et invicem* 2.15, 3.10, 5.47, 57; *Greek Anthology* (*Anthologia Palatina*) 6.227, 261, 345, 9.353, 355; Propertius 3.10; Tibullus 1.7; Apuleius, *Apology* 9.

39. Roche 2011.

40. Fleury 2002.

41. Pernot 2010.

42. On the subject of praise in late antiquity, see, e.g. (among many publications), Brottier 2004; Drake 1976; Grünbart 2007; Hägg and Rousseau 2000; Hürth 1906; MacCormack 1981; Malosse 2000; Marasco 2002; Milazzo 1999, 2003; Pernot 2003; Whitby 1998; Zarini 2005.

43. On this genre, see, e.g., Cogitore and Goyet 2003; Fontani 2007; Pernot 1997:123ff.; Wallace-Hadrill 1981.

44. Theopompus: Jacoby, *Die Fragmente der griechischen Historiker* 115 F 255–258. Lamachus: Plutarch, *Demosthenes* 9.1. Metrodorus and Aesop: Jacoby, *Die Fragmente der griechischen Historiker* 184, 187 a.

45. Jacoby, *Die Fragmente der griechischen Historiker* 147 T 1.

46. Appian, *Civil Wars* 2.144–147; Cassius Dio, *Roman History* 44.36–49, 56.35–41.

47. On the inauthenticity of this speech and the problem of the *laudandus* see Pernot 1997:171–183.

48. On the Latin panegyrics see Nixon and Rodgers 1994; Rees 2002, 2012; Hostein 2012.

49. Cf. the list in Kierdorf 1980:137–149.

50. All these speeches are cited in the *Suda*, respectively A 4203; Ω 189; Z 73; N 404; Π 1951.

51. Pernot 2010:81–83.

52. Drake 1976.

53. Cf. Norman 1969.

54. Guida 1990.

55. Cf. Elm 2012; Lieu 1986.

56. On city encomium, see, e.g., Bouffartigue 1996; Classen 1980; Gernentz 1918; Marasco 2002.

CHAPTER 2: THE GRAMMAR OF PRAISE

1. Green 2010:137.

2. Summary drawn from Russell and Wilson 1981:270, with adaptations.

3. Hawhee 2004.

4. E.g., Quintilian, *The Orator's Education* 3.7.15; Hermogenes, *Preliminary Exercises* 7.16; Menander Rhetor II, 371–372.

5. Example of the first meaning: Hermogenes, *Preliminary Exercises* 7.16; of the second meaning: Menander Rhetor II, 384.

6. Quintilian, *The Orator's Education* 3.7.17–18; Hermogenes, *Preliminary Exercises* 7.16–17.

7. *Phaedo* 69b–c; *Republic* 4.427e–434d; *Laws* 1.630a–631c, 3.688a–b, 12.963a–965e.

8. *Protagoras* 330b, 349b; *Euthyphro* 12e.

9. Hermogenes, *Preliminary Exercises* 7.16; Nicolaus, *Preliminary Exercises* 8.50, 52, 53.

10. On this list and its history, see Woods 2009.

11. Aelius Theon 7(11).118; Hermogenes 10.22; Aphthonius 12.37; Nicolaus 11.68. "Description" (*ekphrasis*) is an important issue in current research on rhetoric: see Webb 2009.

12. Notably Pseudo-Dionysius of Halicarnassus, *Rhetoric* 1.257, 5.275–276; Menander Rhetor I, 344–367; Menander Rhetor II, 382–388, 425–429.

13. Ptolemy, *Geography* 1.1.2.8.

14. E.g., Aelius Theon, *Exercises* 9(8).109.

15. Grandjean 1975.

16. Quintilian, *The Orator's Education* 3.7.7–9; Alexander, son of Numenius, in Spengel 1853–1856:3.4–6; Menander Rhetor I, 333–344. See also Pseudo-Dionysius of Halicarnassus, *Rhetoric* 1.256–257; Menander Rhetor II, 400–402, 438–443.

17. *Orations* 37–46. See also Julian, *Orations* 11; Libanius, *Orations* 5.

18. Cf. Pernot 2005a.

19. Vallozza 2001.

20. Translation of the titles is from Russell and Wilson 1981.

21. Appian, *Civil Wars* 2.146; Cassius Dio, *Roman History* 44.49. Cf. Cicero, *Philippics* 2.90: "That beautiful tribute to the deceased, the pathos,

the incitement—they were yours" (trans. Shackleton Bailey, Ramsey, and Manuwald [2009:143]).

22. See the important chapter *On Pity* (*Peri eleou*) in Apsines' *Rhetoric* (Dilts and Kennedy 1997:206–239).

23. See Menander Rhetor II, 388–394; and Mras 1949; Pernot 1993a:546–568; Stock 1911.

24. See, e.g., Rees 2007.

25. Isocrates, *Against the Sophists* 16, *Panegyricus* 11, *To Philip* 27, *Panathenaicus* 2; Aristotle, *Rhetoric* 3.1414a18–19. On the concept of "Gorgianic figures" see Noël 1999.

26. Pseudo-Dionysius of Halicarnassus, *Rhetoric* 1.260, 2.266, 5.276–277, 6.283; Menander Rhetor I, 335, 336, 337, 339, 342; Menander Rhetor II, 374, 389–390, 399–400, 411–412, 414.

27. Lausberg 1998:338.

28. See Koenen 1970:245–246; Soffel 1974:27, 31, 34.

29. On hyperbole see Lausberg 1998:263–264, 410–411, and two more recent publications: Barsi and Boccali 2010; Johnson 2010.

30. *Rhetoric to Herennius* 4.44; Trypho, *On Tropes* 12 (in Spengel 1853–1856:3.198); Longinus, *On the Sublime* 38; Quintilian, *The Orator's Education* 8.4.29, 8.6.67.

31. As observed by Alexander, son of Numenius, in a text published for the first time by Ballaira (1976:324).

32. Seneca, *Consolation to Polybius* 7, 13; Pliny the Younger, *Panegyricus* 19, 80; Dio Chrysostom, *Orations* 1.24, 71; 3.11, 57, 73–81; 40.15; Menander Rhetor II, 371, 422.

33. Menander Rhetor II, 378, 380, 381.

34. Sophists: Aelius Aristides, Libanius, Apuleius. Consuls: Pliny the Younger, Mamertinus (*Latin Panegyrics* 11). Moralist: Dio Chrysostom. Students: see Menander Rhetor. Pupil: Gregory Thaumaturgus. Ephebe: see *The Oxyrhynchus Papyri* 17.2084 (third century AD). Philosopher: see *Corpus Hermeticum* 18.

35. On blame, invective, vituperation, and polemics in general see Albert and Nicolas 2010; Conley 2010; Koster 1980; Rountree 2001; Spina 2001.

36. See, e.g., Aristotle, *Rhetoric* 1.1368a37; *Rhetoric to Alexander* 3; *Rhetoric to Herennius* 3.10; Cicero, *On the Divisions of Oratory* 70; Quintilian, *The Orator's Education* 3.4.12; Aelius Theon, *Exercises* 9(8).112; Alexander, son of Numenius, in Spengel 1853–1856:3.3; Pseudo-Aelius Aristides, *Rhetoric* 1.160; Menander Rhetor I, 3.

37. *Encomium* 3 and *Invective* 1; *Invectives* 5 and 6.

38. *The Ignorant Book-Collector*, *The Lover of Lies*, and *A Professor of Public Speaking* aim at anonymous targets, while in *Alexander the False Prophet* and *The Passing of Peregrinus* Lucian calls his victims by name. See Jones 1986.

CHAPTER 3: WHY EPIDEICTIC RHETORIC?

1. *Rhetoric* 1, chap. 1–2 (e.g., 1354b16ff., 1357a1–7); 2.1377b20–1378a5, 1391b7–27. For the hypothesis of the afterthought insertion, see Buchheit 1960:118–120.

2. See Oravec 1976; Schirren 2008.

3. Plato, *Sophist* 224b (above, p. 5); Aristotle, *Rhetoric* 1.1358b8 and *passim*.

4. See Hauser 1999.

5. See for instance Theophrastus, cited by Quintilian, *The Orator's Education* 3.7.1; Cicero, *On the Divisions of Oratory* 69.

6. On the multiple meanings of *politikos*, Brandstaetter's study remains valuable (Brandstaetter 1894:133–203). This word is often applied to agonistic (deliberative or judicial) speeches, as opposed to epideictic or sophistic speeches. In other cases, however, *politikos* includes praise (or at least certain forms of praise, those most clearly related to civic interests).

7. Cicero, *On the Orator* 1.141, 2.43, 2.341; Quintilian, *The Orator's Education* 2.4.21, 2.15.20, 3.4.3, 12.2.16.

8. Similarly Quintilian, *The Orator's Education* 3.7.1: "its name, which is derived from the notion of display [*eius nominis quod ab ostentatione ducitur*]."

9. On this linguistic problem see Pernot 1993a:36–37.

10. See, e.g., Aelius Theon, *Exercises* 1.61; Quintilian, *The Orator's Education* 3.4.12–13.

11. Cf. Ziegler 1949:559–571.

12. See Danisch 2006; Garrison 2003; Keränen 2001; Sullivan 1993.

13. See also *Nicomachean Ethics* 10.1178b8–18; *Eudemian Ethics* 2.1219b8–16; *Rhetoric* 1.1367b33–35.

14. E.g., Plato, *Republic* 3.387c–388e; *Laws* 12.947b, 960a; Plutarch, *How to Tell a Flatterer from a Friend* 56a; *On Praising Oneself Inoffensively* 545f; *On Exile* 599b.

15. Savon 1980.

16. Cicero, *Brutus* 62; Livy, *History of Rome* 8.40; Tacitus, *Annals* 13.3.

17. *Menippean Satires* 380 (Cèbe 1990:1548–1609).

18. This definition is repeated in a scholion to Julius Victor's *Ars rhetorica* (Halm 1863:446, app. crit.). It is taken from Lactantius' *Divine Institutes* 1.15 (McDonald 1964:62), adapted and moved away from its original sense: while Lactantius is striking out against the divinization of sovereigns, Isidore and the scholiast of Julius Victor transform his text into a valuable definition for the ensemble of the panegyric genre. For a Byzantine invective against the writers of funeral orations, see Sideras 2002.

19. See Shelton 2013 on women in Pliny's *Letters* and the author's self-portraiture.

20. The *laudandus*'s mother may be mentioned in the encomium of an individual (in accordance with the *topoi* of "origin" and "birth"); the bride in the various forms of epithalamium; and the empress in the Imperial oration. See the mentions of Eteoneus' mother in Aelius Aristides, *Orations* 31.2–3, and Julian's encomium in honor of the empress Eusebia.

21. On the interaction between orator and audience see Korenjak 2000.

22. The precise method of calculation is explained in Pernot 1993a: 454–460.

23. See Dio Chrysostom, *Orations* 19.1–2; 42; 57.2, 11; 72.11–16. Also Jones 1978:28.

24. Pernot 2009.

25. A few instances: Crété 2010; Feissel 1998; Henry 1983; Jones 1997; Lattimore 1942; Neri 1981; Robert 1948, 1977; Stecher 1981; Vérilhac 1978–1982; Wörrle 1995.

26. See the work of Lamp (2013), who proposes that epideictic rhetoric thrived in alternative forms (e.g., monuments, coins) during the Augustan principate. Visual rhetoric is an important issue; see (concerning modern times) Olson 2004 and Olson, Finnegan, and Hope 2008.

27. See Isocrates, *Encomium of Helen* 12 (quoted on p. 37).

28. *Rhetoric to Alexander*, chap. 3; Cicero, *On the Orator* 3.105, *Divisions of Oratory* 71; Quintilian, *The Orator's Education* 2.10.11, 3.4.8, 3.7.6; Aelius Theon, *Exercises* 1.65; Nicolaus, *Preliminary Exercises* 7.37; Sopater, *Commentary to Hermogenes*, in Walz 1832–1836:5.16; rhetorical *prolegomena* by various authors, Rabe 1931:185, 246, 293. On amplification see Plöbst 1911.

29. See an interesting passage on the methodology of comparison in Isocrates, *Panathenaicus* 39–41.

30. Lucian (*In Praise of Demosthenes* 10) mocks this procedure.

31. Cf. Baldwin 1984.

32. See Pernot 2011b:1298–1300.

33. Curtius 1953: chap. 5; Vérilhac 1978–1982:2.19–22.

34. Above, pp. 38–39. Cf. Perelman and Olbrechts-Tyteca 1969:293ff.

35. Webb 2003:134–135: "The epideictic orator was not . . . simply stating the obvious, but was selecting evidence for a certain interpretation of events from a multifarious reality which could be subject to competing interpretations. . . . The epideictic orator has a role which is as dynamic as that of the forensic or deliberative orator."

36. Cf. Marchant, in Marchant and Bowersock 1968: xviii.

37. On the theme of glory in poetry, see Nagy 1979:222–242, 1989:8–18. On the ritual function of epideictic, see Carter 1991.

38. Thucydides 2.43; Lysias, *Orations* 2.79–80; Plato, *Menexenus* 236e; Demosthenes, *Orations* 60.2; Hyperides, *Funeral Oration* 42; Isocrates, *Evagoras* 4; Polybius 6.54; Pliny, *Letters* 3.10; Aelius Aristides, *Orations* 32.3.

39. Aelius Aristides, *Orations* 27.46, 46.3; Pseudo–Dionysius of Halicarnassus, *Rhetoric* 1.255, 2.261, 6.283; Menander Rhetor II, 368, 399, 400.

40. As for exhortation, see Thucydides 2.43ff.; Plato, *Menexenus* 246aff.; Dio Chrysostom, *Orations* 29.21–22; Aelius Aristides, *Orations* 31.19, 32.37–38; Pseudo–Dionysius of Halicarnassus, *Rhetoric* 6.280; Menander Rhetor II, 421.

41. Aristophanes, *Frogs* 1026–1027; Plato, *Protagoras* 326a; Isocrates, *Panegyricus* 159; *Evagoras* 5–6, 76–77; Xenophon, *Memorabilia* 3.5.3, 8ff.; Hyperides, *Funeral Oration* 34; Polybius, *Histories* 6.54; Quintilian, *The Orator's Education* 1.2.21; Pliny the Younger, *Letters* 3.18.2–3; Apuleius, *Florida* 17.18–19; Aelius Aristides, *Orations* 3.575; Julian, *Panegyricus to Eusebia* 103c.

42. For this distinction between *sumboulē* and *parainesis*, see Ammonius, *De vocabulorum differentia* 455 (Nickau 1966); the hypothesis to Isocrates, *To Demonicus* (Mathieu and Brémond 1929–1962:1.122, lines 29–33); Syrianus, *Scholia to Hermogenes* (Rabe 1892–1893:2.192); rhetorical *prolegomena* (ed. Rabe 1931:246). In Latin, the equivalent of *parainesis* in this sense is *exhortatio*, defined as the reinforcing of an already held conviction: see Victorinus, *Commentary to Cicero* (Halm 1863:174, lines 33–37). These distinctions of terminology are not always observed in current usage.

43. So Wuellner 1979:184–185.

44. See Cassin 1991.

45. See Borgognoni 2010.

46. For a discussion of community, microcommunity, and the shaping of community in a modern context, see Condit 1985. See also Thorpe 2014.

47. I owe this remark to Susan Jarratt.

48. See Michel 1982.

CHAPTER 4: NEW APPROACHES IN EPIDEICTIC

1. Austin 1962. For a detailed attempt at applying Austin's theory to the concept of epideictic (without reference to antiquity), see Beale 1978.

2. Russell and Wilson 1981:281.

3. Norman 1969:xxxv.

4. On the problem of the unspoken and innuendo (in various sectors and periods), see, e.g., Ahl 1984; Bartsch 2012a, 2012b; Burrow 2008; Carlos 2010; Dominik, Garthwaite, and Roche 2009; Roche 2011; Sharpe 1987; Strauss 1952. Fumaroli 2002 is particularly important. I have been interested in this issue for the last several years: cf. Pernot 1997, 2008b, 2011a. See also Walzer 2013 and Gehrke et al. 2013 on *parrhēsia.*

5. The main ancient texts on "figured speech" are Demetrius, *On Style* 287–295; Quintilian, *The Orator's Education* 9.2.65–99; Hermogenes or Pseudo-Hermogenes, *On Invention* 4.13 and *On Method of Forceful Speaking* 22 (Kennedy 2005:187–196, 238–241); Pseudo–Dionysius of Halicarnassus, *Rhetoric*, chaps. 8–9; Apsines, *On Figured Problems* (Patillon 2001a:112–121).

6. It was taken seriously by many readers, but only in recent times was it fully recognized (if not by all, at least by a great number of scholars) as being ironical or parodical. See Clavaud 1980, Coventry 1989; Hariman 2008:251–253; Loraux 1986; Méridier 1931:51–82; Tsitsiridis 1998.

7. 101–102 (*In Alcibiades* 104a) (trans. O'Neill [1965:66–67]).

8. In the following pages I am restating some interpretations suggested in Pernot 2008a. See also Bowie 2013.

9. Hermogenes, *On Invention* 4.13 (206) (Kennedy 2005:188–189). On significant silence in general see Montiglio 2000.

10. E.g., Aelius Theon, *Exercises* 1.63, 9(8).110; Dio Chrysostom, *Orations* 77/78.17; Tacitus, *Agricola* 1; Plutarch, *On Praising Oneself Inoffensively* 543d; Aelius Aristides, *Orations* 23.7; Cassius Dio, *Roman History* 44.36.5. See Vallozza 1989.

11. Aristotle also refers to the Platonic passage in *Rhetoric* 1.1367b7–9. See Spina 1999.

12. See Demosthenes, *On the Crown* 128; Apuleius, *Florida* 17.21.

13. See Pernot 1998.

14. See also Philo, *On Dreams* 2.272.

15. See Pernot 2006.

16. See Brucker 1997.

17. On the rhetoric of prayer see FitzGerald 2012.

18. See Kennedy 1998; Detienne 2008; Mao 2013.

19. Some examples of publications on the subject: Braungart 1988; Conley 2002; Granier 2009; Hardison 1962; Hennequin 1977; Kallendorf 1989; Kopperschmidt and Schanze 1999; Lockwood 1996; McManamon 1989; MacPhail 2012; Mary and Sot 2001; O'Malley 1979; Paul 1980; Van der Poel 1996; Vickers 1982–1983, 1983; Walker 2004; Zoberman 1991, 1998.

20. Classen 1992:256. See also Hewett 2010.

21. Respectively, Fox 1983:11; Jensen 1987:221; Abbott 1987:260–261.

22. Hampâté Bâ 1994:28–29 (my translation).

BIBLIOGRAPHY

Abbott, Don P. 1987. "The Ancient Word: Rhetoric in Aztec Culture." *Rhetorica* 5:251–264.

Adler, Ada. 1928–1938. *Suidae Lexicon*. Leipzig: Teubner.

Ahl, Frederick M. 1984. "The Art of Safe Criticism in Greece and Rome." *American Journal of Philology* 105:174–208.

Albert, Luce, and Loïc Nicolas, eds. 2010. *Polémique et rhétorique de l'Antiquité à nos jours*. Brussels: De Boeck/Duculot.

Alexiou, Margaret. 2002. *The Ritual Lament in Greek Tradition*. 2nd ed. Lanham, MD: Rowman and Littlefield.

Alonso del Real, Concepción, ed. 2001. *Consolatio: Nueve estudios*. Pamplona: Universidad de Navarra.

Atwill, Janet M. 1998. *Rhetoric Reclaimed: Aristotle and the Liberal Arts Tradition*. Ithaca, NY: Cornell University Press.

Austin, J. L. 1962. *How to Do Things with Words*. Oxford: Oxford University Press.

Baldwin, Barry. 1984. "The First and Only." *Glotta* 62:58–59.

Ballaira, Guglielmo. 1976. "Una figura inedita del *Περὶ σχημάτων* di Alessandro di Numenio e le sue affinità con Quintiliano (*inst.* 8, 6, 67–76)." *Rheinisches Museum* 119:324–328.

Baltussen, Han, ed. 2013. *Greek and Roman Consolations: Eight Studies of a Tradition and Its Afterlife*. Swansea: Classical Press of Wales.

Barbantani, Silvia. 2001. *Φάτις νικηφόρος: Frammenti di elegia encomiastica nell'età delle Guerre Galatiche*. Supplementum Hellenisticum 958 and 969. Milan: Vita e Pensiero.

Barney, Stephen A., W. J. Lewis, J. A. Beach, and Oliver Berghof. 1996. *The Etymologies of Isidore of Seville*. Cambridge: Cambridge University Press.

Barsi, Monica, and Giuliano Boccali, eds. 2010. *Funzioni e finzioni dell'iperbole tra scienze e lettere*. Milan: Cisalpino.

Bartsch, Shadi. 2012a. "Praise and Doublespeak: Tacitus' *Dialogus.*" In *Oxford Readings in Tacitus*, ed. Rhiannon Ash, 119–154. Oxford: Oxford University Press.

———. 2012b. "The Art of Sincerity: Pliny's *Panegyricus.*" In *Latin Panegyric*, ed. Roger Rees, 148–193. Oxford: Oxford University Press.

Beale, Walter H. 1978. "Rhetorical Performative Discourse: A New Theory of Epideictic." *Philosophy and Rhetoric* 11:221–246.

Behr, Charles A. 1981–1986. *P. Aelius Aristides: The Complete Works.* Leiden: Brill.

Bérenger, Agnès, and Éric Perrin-Saminadayar, eds. 2009. *Les entrées royales et impériales: Histoire, représentation et diffusion d'une cérémonie publique, de l'Orient ancien à Byzance.* Paris: De Boccard.

Bompaire, Jacques. 1958. *Lucien écrivain: Imitation et création.* Paris: De Boccard.

Borgognoni, Rocco. 2010. "Parlare alle istituzioni, parlare delle istituzioni: Retorica, verità e persuasione nell'Oriente tardoantico." In *Istituzioni, carismi ed esercizio del potere (IV–VI secolo d.C.)*, ed. Giorgio Bonamente and Rita Lizzi Testa, 77–90. Bari: Edipuglia.

Bouffartigue, Jean. 1996. "La tradition de l'éloge de la cité dans le monde grec." In *La fin de la cité antique et le début de la cité médiévale de la fin du IIIe siècle à l'avènement de Charlemagne*, ed. Claude Lepelley, 43–58. Bari: Edipuglia.

Bowie, Ewen L. 1989a. "Greek Sophists and Greek Poetry in the Second Sophistic." *Aufstieg und Niedergang der römischen Welt* 2.33.1:209–258.

———. 1989b. "Poetry and Poets in Asia and Achaia." In *The Greek Renaissance in the Roman Empire*, ed. Susan Walker and Averil Cameron, 189–205. Bulletin of the Institute of Classical Studies, suppl. 55. London: Institute of Classical Studies.

———. 1990. "Greek Poetry in the Antonine Age." In *Antonine Literature*, ed. Donald A. Russell, 53–90. Oxford: Clarendon Press.

———. 2002. "Sympotic Praise." *Gaia* 6:169–199.

———. 2013. "I discorsi civici di Elio Aristide." In *Elio Aristide e la legittimazione greca dell'impero di Roma*, ed. Paolo Desideri and Francesca Fontanella, 69–89. Bologna: Il Mulino.

Brandstaetter, Karl. 1894. "De notionum πολιτικός et σοφιστής usu rhetorico." *Leipziger Studien zur classischen Philologie* 15:129–274.

Braungart, Georg. 1988. *Hofberedsamkeit: Studien zur Praxis höfisch-politischer Rede im deutschen Territorialabsolutismus.* Tübingen: Niemeyer.

Brottier, Laurence. 2004. *Figures de l'évêque idéal: Jean Chrysostome, Panégy-*

rique de saint Mélèce. Jean Damascène, Panégyrique de saint Jean Chrysostome. Paris: Les Belles Lettres.

Brucker, Ralph. 1997. *"Christushymnen" oder "epideiktische Passagen"? Studien zum Stilwechsel im Neuen Testament und seiner Umwelt.* Göttingen: Vandenhoeck and Ruprecht.

Buchheit, Vinzenz. 1960. *Untersuchungen zur Theorie des Genos Epideiktikon von Gorgias bis Aristoteles.* Munich: Hueber.

Burgess, Theodore C. 1902. "Epideictic Literature." *University of Chicago Studies in Classical Philology* 3:87–263.

Burrow, John A. 2008. *The Poetry of Praise.* Cambridge: Cambridge University Press.

Cairns, Francis. 2007. *Generic Composition in Greek and Roman Poetry. Corrected, with New Material.* Ann Arbor: Michigan Classical Press.

Cameron, Averil. 1991. *Christianity and the Rhetoric of Empire: The Development of Christian Discourse.* Berkeley: University of California Press.

Carey, Christopher. 2007. "Epideictic Oratory." In Worthington 2007: 236–252.

Carlos, Claudia. 2010. "Techniques of Bold Speaking, Safely, in Bossuet's 'Sermon sur la prédication évangélique' (1662)." *Rhetorica* 28:197–221.

Carter, Michael F. 1991. "The Ritual Functions of Epideictic Rhetoric: The Case of Socrates' Funeral Oration." *Rhetorica* 9:209–232.

Cary, Earnest. 1914–1927. *Dio's Roman History.* London: Heinemann; Cambridge, MA: Harvard University Press.

Cassin, Barbara. 1991. "Consensus et création des valeurs: Qu'est-ce qu'un éloge?" In *Les Grecs, les Romains et nous: L'Antiquité est-elle moderne?*, ed. Roger-Pol Droit, 273–299. Paris: Le Monde Éditions.

———. 1995. *L'effet sophistique.* Paris: Gallimard.

Cazzaniga, Ignazio, and Mariangela Vandoni. 1957. "Frammenti di *encomia* a Minosse, Radamante e Tideo." *Studi italiani di filologia classica*, n.s., 29:133–173.

Cèbe, Jean-Pierre. 1990. *Varron: Satires Ménippées* 9. Rome: École française de Rome.

Charbonnel, Nanine. 1997. "Éloge de l'éloge." In *Le don de la parole: Mélanges offerts à Daniel Hameline pour son soixante-quinzième anniversaire*, ed. Nanine Charbonnel, 1–11. Bern: Lang.

Chase, J. Richard. 1961. "The Classical Conception of Epideictic." *Quarterly Journal of Speech* 47:293–300.

Chiron, Pierre. 2002. *Pseudo-Aristote: Rhétorique à Alexandre.* Paris: Les Belles Lettres.

Clark, Donald L. 1957. *Rhetoric in Greco-Roman Education.* New York: Columbia University Press.

Classen, Carl Joachim. 1980. *Die Stadt im Spiegel der Descriptiones und Laudes urbium in der antiken und mittelalterlichen Literatur bis zum Ende des zwölften Jahrhunderts.* Hildesheim: Olms.

———. 1992. "Die Rhetorik im öffentlichen Leben unserer Zeit." In *Die Macht des Wortes: Aspekte gegenwärtiger Rhetorikforschung,* ed. Carl Joachim Classen and Heinz-Joachim Müllenbrock, 247–267. Marburg: Hitzeroth.

Clavaud, Robert. 1980. *Le Ménéxène de Platon et la rhétorique de son temps.* Paris: Les Belles Lettres.

Cogitore, Isabelle, and Francis Goyet, eds. 2003. *L'éloge du Prince: De l'Antiquité au temps des Lumières.* Grenoble: Ellug.

Cohoon, James W., and Henry Lamar Crosby. 1932–1951. *Dio Chrysostom.* London: Heinemann; Cambridge, MA: Harvard University Press.

Colson, F. H., and G. H. Whitaker. 1929–1943. *Philo.* London: Heinemann; Cambridge, MA: Harvard University Press.

Condit, Celeste Michelle. 1985. "The Functions of Epideictic: The Boston Massacre Orations as Exemplar." *Communication Quarterly* 33:284–299.

Conley, Thomas M. 1990. *Rhetoric in the European Tradition.* Chicago: University of Chicago Press.

———. 2002. "The Speech of Ibrahim at the Coronation of Maximilian II." *Rhetorica* 20:263–273.

———. 2010. *Toward a Rhetoric of Insult.* Chicago: University of Chicago Press.

Consigny, Scott. 2001. *Gorgias: Sophist and Artist.* Columbia: University of South Carolina Press.

Copenhaver, Brian P. 1992. *Hermetica: The Greek Corpus Hermeticum and the Latin Asclepius.* Cambridge: Cambridge University Press.

Coventry, Lucinda J. 1989. "Philosophy and Rhetoric in the *Menexenus.*" *Journal of Hellenic Studies* 109:1–15.

Crété, Moira. 2010. "Les formes de l'éloge dans les inscriptions honorifiques du Latium et de la Campanie (IIe–IVe siècle ap. J.-C.)." *Mélanges de l'École française de Rome: Antiquité* 122:191–226.

Cribiore, Raffaella. 2001. *Gymnastics of the Mind: Greek Education in Hellenistic and Roman Egypt.* Princeton: Princeton University Press.

Curtius, Ernst Robert. 1953. *European Literature and the Latin Middle Ages.* Trans. Willard R. Trask. New York: Pantheon Books; London: Routledge and Kegan Paul.

Dagron, Gilbert. 2007. *Décrire et peindre: Essai sur le portrait iconique*. Paris: Gallimard.

Dandrey, Patrick. 1997. *L'éloge paradoxal de Gorgias à Molière*. Paris: Presses Universitaires de France.

Danisch, Robert. 2006. "Power and the Celebration of the Self: Michel Foucault's Epideictic Rhetoric." *Southern Communication Journal* 71:291–307.

Davies, Malcolm, and Sarah B. Pomeroy. 2012. "Marcellus of Side's Epitaph on Regilla (*IG* XIV 1389): An Historical and Literary Commentary." *Prometheus* 38:3–34.

Demont, Paul. 1993. "Die *Epideixis* über die *Techne* im V. und IV. Jh." In *Vermittlung und Tradierung von Wissen in der griechischen Kultur*, ed. Wolfgang Kullmann and Jochen Althoff, 181–209. Tübingen: Narr.

Detienne, Marcel. 2008. *Comparing the Incomparable*. Trans. Janet Lloyd. Stanford, CA: Stanford University Press.

Dilts, Mervin R., and George A. Kennedy. 1997. *Two Greek Rhetorical Treatises from the Roman Empire: Introduction, Text, and Translation of the Arts of Rhetoric Attributed to Anonymous Seguerianus and to Apsines of Gadara*. Leiden: Brill.

Di Nanni Durante, Diva. 2007–2008. "I Sebastà di Neapolis: Il regolamento e il programma." *Ludica* 13–14:7–22.

Dominicy, Marc, and Madeleine Frédéric, eds. 2001. *La mise en scène des valeurs: La rhétorique de l'éloge et du blâme*. Lausanne: Delachaux and Niestlé.

Dominik, William J., John Garthwaite, and Paul A. Roche, eds. 2009. *Writing Politics in Imperial Rome*. Leiden: Brill.

Drake, Harold Allen. 1976. *In Praise of Constantine: A Historical Study and New Translation of Eusebius' Tricennial Orations*. Berkeley: University of California Press.

Duffy, Bernard K. 1983. "The Platonic Functions of Epideictic Rhetoric." *Philosophy and Rhetoric* 16:79–93.

Dufraigne, Pierre. 1994. *Adventus Augusti, adventus Christi: Recherche sur l'exploitation idéologique et littéraire d'un cérémonial dans l'Antiquité tardive*. Paris: Institut d'Études Augustiniennes.

Durry, Marcel. 1942. "*Laudatio funebris* et rhétorique." *Revue de Philologie* 68:105–114.

Elm, Susanna. 2012. *Sons of Hellenism, Fathers of the Church: Emperor Julian, Gregory of Nazianzus, and the Vision of Rome*. Berkeley: University of California Press.

Ernst, Paul. 2012. "L'arrivée de Caton le Jeune à Antioche dans les récits de

Plutarque et de Julien: Des discours, une pratique et des représentations." *Revue des Études Grecques* 125:443–72.

Esteve Forriol, José. 1962. *Die Trauer- und Trostgedichte in der römischen Literatur untersucht nach ihrer Topik und ihrem Motivschatz*. Munich: Schubert.

Favez, Charles. 1937. *La consolation latine chrétienne*. Paris: Vrin.

Feissel, Denis. 1998. "Gouverneurs et édifices dans des épigrammes de Smyrne au Bas-Empire." *Revue des Études Grecques* 111:125–144.

FitzGerald, William. 2012. *Spiritual Modalities: Prayer as Rhetoric and Performance*. University Park: Penn State Press.

Fleury, Pascale. 2002. "L'éloge paradoxal, entre virtuosité et construction idéologique: Le cas de l'*Éloge de la négligence* de Fronton." *Rhetorica* 20: 119–132.

Foerster, Richard, and Eberhard Richtsteig. 1903–1927. *Libanii Opera*. Leipzig: Teubner.

Follet, Simone. 1976. *Athènes au IIe et au IIIe siècle: Études chronologiques et prosopographiques*. Paris: Les Belles Lettres.

Fontani, Enrica. 2007. "La celebrazione dell'imperatore nelle feste in onore di Adriano nell'Oriente greco." In *Arte e memoria culturale nell'età della Seconda Sofistica*, ed. Orietta Dora Cordovana and Marco Galli, 235–240. Catania: Edizioni del Prisma.

Fowler, Harold N. 1921. *Plato: Theaetetus. Sophist*. London: Heinemann; Cambridge, MA: Harvard University Press.

Fowler, Robert L. 1987. "The Rhetoric of Desperation." *Harvard Studies in Classical Philology* 91:5–38.

Fox, Michael V. 1983. "Ancient Egyptian Rhetoric." *Rhetorica* 1:9–22.

Fraustadt, Georg. 1909. *Encomiorum in litteris Graecis usque ad Romanam aetatem historia*. Leipzig: Noske.

Fumaroli, Marc. 1980. *L'âge de l'éloquence: Rhétorique et "res literaria" de la Renaissance au seuil de l'époque classique*. Geneva: Droz.

———, ed. 1999. *Histoire de la rhétorique dans l'Europe moderne, 1450–1950*. Paris: Presses Universitaires de France.

———. 2002. *The Poet and the King: Jean de La Fontaine and His Century*. Trans. Jane Marie Todd. Notre Dame, IN: University of Notre Dame Press.

Furley, William D. 1995. "Praise and Persuasion in Greek Hymns." *Journal of Hellenic Studies* 115:29–46.

Furley, William D., and Jan Maarten Bremer. 2001. *Greek Hymns: Selected Cult Songs from the Archaic to the Hellenistic Period*. Tübingen: Mohr Siebeck.

Gangloff, Anne. 2009. "La constitution du mythe en genre rhétorique: Les hymnes chez Alexandre, fils de Nouménios, et chez Ménandre le Rhéteur." In *Formes de l'écriture, figures de la pensée dans la culture gréco-romaine*, ed. Françoise Toulze-Morisset, 3:19–31. Villeneuve-d'Ascq: Université Charles-de-Gaulle–Lille.

Garrison, Jim. 2003. "Prophetic Epideictic Rhetoric: Poetic Education beyond Good and Evil." *Educational Theory* 53:221–241.

Garver, Eugene. 2009. "Aristotle on the Kinds of Rhetoric." *Rhetorica* 27: 1–18.

Garzya, Antonio. 1983. *Il mandarino e il quotidiano: Saggi sulla letteratura tardoantica e bizantina*. Naples: Bibliopolis.

Gehrke, Pat J., Susan C. Jarratt, Bradford Vivian, and Arthur E. Walzer. 2013. "Forum on Arthur Walzer's '*Parrēsia*, Foucault, and the Classical Rhetorical Tradition.'" *Rhetoric Society Quarterly* 43:355–381.

Gernentz, Wilhelm. 1918. *Laudes Romae*. Rostock: Adler.

Gibson, Craig A. 2008. *Libanius's Progymnasmata: Model Exercises in Greek Prose Composition and Rhetoric*. Atlanta: Society of Biblical Literature.

Giombini, Stefania. 2012. *Gorgia epidittico: Commento filosofico all'Encomio di Elena, all'Apologia di Palamede, all'Epitafio*. Passignano sul Trasimeno: Aguaplano.

Gödde, Susanne. 2011. *Euphêmia: Die gute Rede in Kult und Literatur der griechischen Antike*. Heidelberg: Winter.

Goeken, Johann. 2012. *Aelius Aristide et la rhétorique de l'hymne en prose*. Turnhout: Brepols.

Grandjean, Yves. 1975. *Une nouvelle arétalogie d'Isis à Maronée*. Leiden: Brill.

Granier, Thomas. 2009. "La *renovatio* du modèle rhétorique antique dans les éloges urbains de l'Italie du haut Moyen Âge." In *Au Moyen Âge: Entre tradition antique et innovation*, ed. Michel Balard and Michel Sot, 35–56. Paris: Comité des Travaux Historiques et Scientifiques.

Green, Lawrence D. 2010. "Renaissance Views of Aristotelian Topoi." In *Papers on Rhetoric, X*, ed. Lucia Calboli Montefusco, 127–139. Rome: Herder.

Grünbart, Michael, ed. 2007. *Theatron: Rhetorische Kultur in Spätantike und Mittelalter / Rhetorical Culture in Late Antiquity and the Middle Ages*. Berlin: De Gruyter.

Guida, Augusto. 1990. *Un anonimo panegirico per l'imperatore Giuliano*. Florence: Olschki.

Guipponi-Gineste, Marie-France. 2010. *Claudien: Poète du monde à la cour d'Occident*. Paris: De Boccard.

Gunderson, Erik. 2000. *Staging Masculinity: The Rhetoric of Performance in the Roman World*. Ann Arbor: University of Michigan Press.

Hägg, Thomas, and Philip Rousseau, eds. 2000. *Greek Biography and Panegyric in Late Antiquity*. Berkeley: University of California Press.

Halfmann, Helmut. 1986. *Itinera Principum: Geschichte und Typologie der Kaiserreisen im römischen Reich*. Stuttgart: Steiner.

Halliwell, Stephen, W. H. Fyfe, Donald A. Russell, and Doreen C. Innes. 1995. *Aristotle: Poetics. Longinus: On the Sublime. Demetrius: On Style*. Cambridge, MA: Harvard University Press.

Halm, Karl. 1863. *Rhetores Latini Minores*. Leipzig: Teubner.

Hampâté Bâ, Amadou. 1994. *Oui mon commandant! Mémoires (II)*. Paris: Actes Sud.

Hardie, Alex. 1983. *Statius and the Silvae: Poets, Patrons, and Epideixis in the Graeco-Roman World*. Liverpool: Cairns.

Hardison, Osborne B., Jr. 1962. *The Enduring Monument: A Study of the Idea of Praise in Renaissance Literary Theory*. Chapel Hill: University of North Carolina Press.

Hariman, Robert. 2008. "Political Parody and Public Culture." *Quarterly Journal of Speech* 94:247–272.

Harmon, Austin M., K. Kilburn, and Matthew D. Macleod. 1913–1967. *Lucian*. London: Heinemann; Cambridge, MA: Harvard University Press.

Harrison, Stephen. 2000. *Apuleius: A Latin Sophist*. Oxford: Oxford University Press.

———, ed. 2001. *Apuleius: Rhetorical Works*. Trans. and ed. Stephen Harrison, John Hilton, and Vincent Hunink. Oxford: Oxford University Press.

Hauser, Gerard A. 1999. "Aristotle on Epideictic: The Formation of Public Morality." *Rhetoric Society Quarterly* 29:5–23.

Hawhee, Debra. 2004. *Bodily Arts: Rhetoric and Athletics in Ancient Greece*. Austin: University of Texas Press.

Heath, Malcolm. 2004. *Menander: A Rhetor in Context*. Oxford: Oxford University Press.

Hendrickson, George L., and Harry M. Hubbell. 1939. *Cicero: Brutus. Orator*. London: Heinemann; Cambridge, MA: Harvard University Press.

Hennequin, Jacques. 1977. *Henri IV dans ses oraisons funèbres; ou, La naissance d'une légende*. Paris: Klincksieck.

Henry, Alan S. 1983. *Honours and Privileges in Athenian Decrees: The Principal Formulae of Athenian Honorary Decrees*. Hildesheim: Olms.

Hewett, Beth L. 2010. *Good Words: Memorializing through a Eulogy*. Omaha, NE: Grief Illustrated.

Hinks, D. A. G. 1936. "Tria Genera Causarum." *Classical Quarterly* 30: 170–176.

Holst-Warhaft, Gail. 1992. *Dangerous Voices: Women's Laments and Greek Literature*. London: Routledge.

Horstmann, Sabine. 2004. *Das Epithalamium in der lateinischen Literatur der Spätantike*. Munich: Saur.

Hostein, Antony. 2012. *La cité et l'empereur: Les Éduens dans l'Empire romain d'après les Panégyriques latins*. Paris: Publications de la Sorbonne.

Hunter, Richard. 2003. *Theocritus: Encomium of Ptolemy Philadelphus*. Berkeley: University of California Press.

Hürth, Xavier. 1906. *De Gregorii Nazianzeni orationibus funebribus*. Strasbourg: Truebner.

Jarratt, Susan C. 1991. *Rereading the Sophists: Classical Rhetoric Refigured*. Carbondale: Southern Illinois University Press.

Jasper, David, and Ronald C. D. Jasper, eds. 1990. *Language and the Worship of the Church*. Houndmills, UK: Macmillan.

Jensen, J. Vernon. 1987. "Rhetorical Emphases of Taoism." *Rhetorica* 5: 219–229.

Johann, Horst-Theodor. 1968. *Trauer und Trost: Eine quellen- und strukturanalytische Untersuchung der philosophischen Trostschriften über den Tod*. Munich: Fink.

Johnson, Christopher D. 2010. *Hyperboles: The Rhetoric of Excess in Baroque Literature and Thought*. Cambridge, MA: Harvard University Press.

Johnson, William A., and Daniel S. Richter, eds. Forthcoming. *The Oxford Handbook to the Second Sophistic*. New York: Oxford University Press.

Jones, Christopher P. 1978. *The Roman World of Dio Chrysostom*. Cambridge, MA: Harvard University Press.

———. 1986. *Culture and Society in Lucian*. Cambridge, MA: Harvard University Press.

———. 1997. "Epigrams from Hierapolis and Aphrodisias." *Hermes* 125: 203–214.

———. 2005. *Philostratus: The Life of Apollonius of Tyana*. Cambridge, MA: Harvard University Press.

Jouanna, Jacques. 2012. "Rhetoric and Medicine in the Hippocratic Corpus: A Contribution to the History of Rhetoric in the Fifth Century." In *Greek Medicine from Hippocrates to Galen: Selected Papers*, 39–53. Leiden: Brill.

Kallendorf, Craig. 1989. *In Praise of Aeneas: Virgil and Epideictic Rhetoric in the Early Italian Renaissance.* Hanover, NH: University Press of New England.

Kassel, Rudolf. 1958. *Untersuchungen zur griechischen und römischen Konsolationsliteratur.* Munich: Beck.

Kennedy, George A. 1963. *The Art of Persuasion in Greece.* Princeton: Princeton University Press.

———. 1972. *The Art of Rhetoric in the Roman World: 300 BC–AD 300.* Princeton: Princeton University Press.

———. 1980. *Classical Rhetoric and Its Christian and Secular Tradition from Ancient to Modern Times.* Chapel Hill: University of North Carolina Press.

———. 1983. *Greek Rhetoric under Christian Emperors.* Princeton: Princeton University Press.

———. 1984. *New Testament Interpretation through Rhetorical Criticism.* Chapel Hill: University of North Carolina Press.

———. 1991. *Aristotle, On Rhetoric: A Theory of Civic Discourse.* New York: Oxford University Press.

———. 1998. *Comparative Rhetoric: An Historical and Cross-Cultural Introduction.* New York: Oxford University Press.

———. 2003. *Progymnasmata: Greek Textbooks of Prose Composition and Rhetoric.* Atlanta: Society of Biblical Literature.

———. 2005. *Invention and Method: Two Rhetorical Treatises from the Hermogenic Corpus.* Atlanta: Society of Biblical Literature.

Keränen, Lisa. 2001. "The Hippocratic Oath as Epideictic Rhetoric: Reanimating Medicine's Past for Its Future." *Journal of Medical Humanities* 22:55–68.

Kierdorf, Wilhelm. 1980. *Laudatio Funebris: Interpretationen und Untersuchungen zur Entwicklung der römischen Leichenrede.* Meisenheim am Glan: Hain.

Koenen, Ludwig. 1970. "Die 'Laudatio funebris' des Augustus für Agrippa auf einem neuen Papyrus (P. Colon. inv. Nr. 4701)." *Zeitschrift für Papyrologie und Epigraphik* 5:217–283.

Kopperschmidt, Josef, and Helmut Schanze, eds. 1999. *Fest und Festrhetorik: Zu Theorie, Geschichte und Praxis der Epideiktik.* Munich: Fink.

Korenjak, Martin. 2000. *Publikum und Redner: Ihre Interaktion in der sophistischen Rhetorik der Kaiserzeit.* Munich: Beck.

Koster, Severin. 1980. *Die Invektive in der griechischen und römischen Literatur.* Meisenheim am Glan: Hain.

Kovacs, David. 1995. *Euripides: Children of Heracles. Hippolytus. Andromache. Hecuba*. Cambridge, MA: Harvard University Press.

———. 2002. *Euripides: Bacchae. Iphigenia at Aulis. Rhesus*. Cambridge, MA: Harvard University Press.

La Bua, Giuseppe. 1999. *L'inno nella letterature poetica latina*. San Severo: Gerni.

Lamb, Walter R. M. 1925. *Plato 3: Lysis—Symposium—Gorgias*. Cambridge, MA: Harvard University Press.

Lamp, Kathleen. 2013. *A City of Marble: The Rhetoric of Augustan Rome*. Columbia: University of South Carolina Press.

Lattimore, Richmond. 1942. "Themes in Greek and Latin Epitaphs." *Illinois Studies in Language and Literature* 28, nos. 1–2.

Lausberg, Heinrich. 1998. *Handbook of Literary Rhetoric: A Foundation for Literary Study*. Trans. Matthew T. Bliss, Annemiek Jansen, and David E. Orton. Leiden: Brill.

Lauxtermann, Marc D. 1998. "What Is an Epideictic Epigram?" *Mnemosyne*, ser. 4, 51:525–537.

Leff, Michael. 2009. "The Expedient, the Honorable, and the Sacred: Rhetorical *Topoi* and the Religious Imperative." In *New Chapters in the History of Rhetoric*, ed. Laurent Pernot, 401–413. Leiden: Brill.

Le Guen, Brigitte, ed. 2010. *L'argent dans les concours du monde grec*. Saint-Denis: Presses Universitaires de Vincennes.

Lehmann, Yves, ed. 2007. *L'hymne antique et son public*. Turnhout: Brepols.

Lévy, Carlos. 2001. "Cicéron et l'épicurisme: La problématique de l'éloge paradoxal." In *Cicéron et Philodème: La polémique en philosophie*, ed. Clara Auvray-Assayas and Daniel Delattre, 61–75. Paris: Éditions ENS Rue d'Ulm.

Lieu, Samuel N. C. 1986. *The Emperor Julian: Panegyric and Polemic. Claudius Mamertinus—John Chrysostom—Ephrem the Syrian*. Liverpool: Liverpool University Press.

Lockwood, Richard. 1996. *The Reader's Figure: Epideictic Rhetoric in Plato, Aristotle, Bossuet, Racine, and Pascal*. Geneva: Droz.

Loraux, Nicole. 1986. *The Invention of Athens: The Funeral Oration in the Classical City*. Cambridge, MA: Harvard University Press.

MacCormack, Sabine G. 1972. "Change and Continuity in Late Antiquity: The Ceremony of *Adventus*." *Historia* 21:721–752.

———. 1981. *Art and Ceremony in Late Antiquity*. Berkeley: University of California Press.

MacDonald, Coll. 1976. *Cicero: In Catilinam I–IV. Pro Murena. Pro*

Sulla. Pro Flacco. Cambridge, MA: Harvard University Press; London: Heinemann.

MacDowell, Douglas M. 1982. *Gorgias: Encomium of Helen.* Bristol: Bristol Classical Press.

MacPhail, Eric. 2012. "Philosophers in the New World: Montaigne and the Tradition of Epideictic Rhetoric." *Rhetorica* 30:22–36.

Macrides, Ruth. 2007. *George Akropolites: The History.* Oxford: Oxford University Press.

Maehler, Herwig. 2002. "'Elogio del cavallo' nel P. Oxy. 4647." *Seminari romani di cultura greca* 5:239–53.

Malherbe, Abraham J. 1988. *Ancient Epistolary Theorists.* Atlanta: Scholars Press.

Malosse, Pierre-Louis. 2000. "Sans mentir (ou presque): La dissimulation des faits gênants dans la rhétorique de l'éloge, d'après l'exemple des discours royaux de Libanios." *Rhetorica* 18:243–263.

Malraux, André. 1971. *Oraisons funèbres.* Paris: Gallimard.

Manieri, Alessandra. 2010–2011. "Concorsi a premi e gerarchia sociale degli artisti." *Rudiae* 22–23:659–678.

Mao, LuMing, ed. 2013. *Comparative Rhetoric.* Special issue, *Rhetoric Society Quarterly* 43, no. 3.

Marasco, Gabriele. 2002. "La fondation et les débuts de Constantinople: Éloge et *psogos* dans la tradition contemporaine." In *Études de démographie du monde gréco-romain*, ed. Wiesław Suder, 79–96. Wrocław: Wydawnictwo Uniwersytetu Wrocławskiego.

Marchant, Edgar C., and Glen W. Bowersock. 1968. *Xenophon* 7. London: Heinemann; Cambridge, MA: Harvard University Press.

Martino, Ernesto de. 1958. *Morte e pianto rituale nel mondo antico: Dal lamento pagano al pianto di Maria.* Turin: Einaudi.

Mary, Lionel, and Michel Sot, eds. 2001. *Le discours d'éloge entre Antiquité et Moyen Âge.* Paris: Picard.

Mathieu, Georges, and Émile Brémond. 1929–1962. *Isocrate: Discours.* Paris: Les Belles Lettres.

Matuschek, Stefan. 2001. "Lobrede." In Ueding 1992–2012:5.390–398.

McDonald, Mary Francis. 1964. *Lactantius: The Divine Institutes, Books I–VII.* Washington, DC: Catholic University of America Press.

McManamon, John M. 1989. *Funeral Oratory and the Cultural Ideals of Italian Humanism.* Chapel Hill: University of North Carolina Press.

Méridier, Louis. 1931. *Platon: Œuvres complètes 5.1. Ion—Ménexène—Euthydème.* Paris: Les Belles Lettres.

Meritt, Benjamin Dean. 1931. *Greek Inscriptions, 1896–1927*. Corinth 8.1. Cambridge, MA: Harvard University Press.

Michel, Alain. 1982. *La parole et la beauté: Rhétorique et esthétique dans la tradition occidentale*. Paris: Les Belles Lettres.

Miguélez Cavero, Laura. 2008. *Poems in Context: Greek Poetry in the Egyptian Thebaid, 200–600 AD*. Berlin: De Gruyter.

Milazzo, Antonino M. 1999. "Un'epistola encomiastica di Cassiodoro (*Var.* 10, 3): *Speculum principis* o manierismo retorico?" *Cassiodorus* 5:277–288.

———. 2003. "Un esempio di μοιχείας ἰγκώμιον nelle 'Omelie' pseudoclementine." In *"Munera amicitiae": Studi di storia e cultura sulla Tarda Antichità offerti a Salvatore Pricoco*, ed. Rossana Barcellona and Teresa Sardella, 265–281. Soveria Mannelli: Rubbettino.

Miranda De Martino, Elena. 2007. "Neapolis e gli imperatori: Nuovi dati dai cataloghi dei Sebastà." *Oebalus* 2:203–215.

Mirhady, David C. 1994. "Aristotle, the *Rhetorica ad Alexandrum* and the *tria genera causarum*." In *Peripatetic Rhetoric after Aristotle*, ed. William W. Fortenbaugh and David C. Mirhady, 54–65. New Brunswick, NJ: Transaction.

Mirhady, David C., and Yun Lee Too. 2000. *Isocrates I*. Austin: University of Texas Press.

Montiglio, Silvia. 2000. *Silence in the Land of Logos*. Princeton: Princeton University Press.

Moore, Clifford H., and John Jackson. 1931. *Tacitus: The Histories, Books IV–V. The Annals, Books I–III*. London: Heinemann; Cambridge, MA: Harvard University Press.

Mras, Karl. 1949. "Die προλαλιά bei den griechischen Schriftstellern." *Wiener Studien* 64:71–81.

Murphy, James J., and Richard A. Katula. 1995. *A Synoptic History of Classical Rhetoric*. 2nd ed. Davis, CA: Hermagoras.

Nagy, Gregory. 1979. *The Best of the Achaeans: Concepts of the Hero in Archaic Greek Poetry*. Baltimore, MD: Johns Hopkins University Press.

———. 1986. "Ancient Greek Epic and Praise Poetry: Some Typological Considerations." In *Oral Tradition in Literature: Interpretation in Context*, ed. Foley John Miles, 89–102. Columbia: University of Missouri Press.

———. 1989. "Early Greek Views of Poets and Poetry." In *The Cambridge History of Literary Criticism*, vol. 1: *Classical Criticism*, ed. George A. Kennedy, 1–77. Cambridge: Cambridge University Press.

Neri, Valerio. 1981. "L'elogio della cultura e l'elogio delle virtù politiche nell'epigrafia latina del IV secolo d.C." *Epigraphica* 43:175–201.

Nickau, Klaus. 1966. *Ammonii qui dicitur liber De adfinium vocabulorum differentia*. Leipzig: Teubner.

Nicolas, Loïc. 2009. "La fonction héroïque: Parole épidictique et enjeux de qualification." *Rhetorica* 27:115–141.

Nixon, Charles E. V., and Barbara Saylor Rodgers. 1994. *In Praise of Later Roman Emperors: The Panegyrici Latini*. Berkeley: University of California Press.

Noël, Marie-Pierre. 1999. "Gorgias et l'invention des γοργίεια σχήματα." *Revue des Études Grecques* 112:193–211.

Norden, Eduard. 1899. "Ein Panegyricus auf Augustus in Vergils Aeneis." *Rheinisches Museum für Philologie* 54:466–482.

———. 1918. *Die antike Kunstprosa vom VI. Jahrhundert v. Chr. bis in die Zeit der Renaissance*. 3rd ed. Leipzig: Teubner.

Norman, Albert F. 1969. *Libanius: Selected Works*, vol. 1: *The Julianic Orations*. London: Heinemann; Cambridge, MA: Harvard University Press.

———. 1992. *Libanius: Autobiography and Selected Letters*. Cambridge, MA: Harvard University Press.

Ochs, Donovan J. 1993. *Consolatory Rhetoric: Grief, Symbol, and Ritual in the Greco-Roman Era*. Columbia: University of South Carolina Press.

Oldfather, William A. 1925–1928. *Epictetus: The Discourses as Reported by Arrian, the Manual, and Fragments*. London: Heinemann; Cambridge, MA: Harvard University Press.

Olson, Lester C. 2004. *Benjamin Franklin's Vision of American Community: A Study in Rhetorical Iconology*. Columbia: University of South Carolina Press.

Olson, Lester C., Cara A. Finnegan, and Diane S. Hope, eds. 2008. *Visual Rhetoric: A Reader in Communication and American Culture*. Newbury Park, CA: Sage.

O'Malley, John W. 1979. *Praise and Blame in Renaissance Rome: Rhetoric, Doctrine, and Reform in the Sacred Orators of the Papal Court, c. 1450–1521*. Durham, NC: Duke University Press.

O'Neill, William. 1965. *Proclus: Alcibiades I*. The Hague: Nijhoff.

Oravec, Christine. 1976. "'Observation' in Aristotle's Theory of Epideictic." *Philosophy and Rhetoric* 9:162–174.

Papillon, Terry L. 2004. *Isocrates II*. Austin: University of Texas Press.

Patillon, Michel. 2001a. *Apsinès: Art rhétorique. Problèmes*. Paris: Les Belles Lettres.

———. 2001b. *Longin: Fragments. Rufus: Art rhétorique.* Paris: Les Belles Lettres.

———. 2002. *Pseudo–Aelius Aristide: Arts rhétoriques.* Paris: Les Belles Lettres.

Paul, C. B. 1980. *Science and Immortality: The Éloges of the Paris Academy of Sciences (1699–1791).* Berkeley: University of California Press.

Pease, Arthur S. 1926. "Things without Honor." *Classical Philology* 21:27–42.

Penella, Robert J. 2007. *Man and the Word: The Orations of Himerius.* Berkeley: University of California Press.

Pepe, Cristina. 2013. *The Genres of Rhetorical Speeches in Greek and Roman Antiquity.* Leiden: Brill.

Perelman, Chaïm, and L. Olbrechts-Tyteca. 1969. *The New Rhetoric: A Treatise on Argumentation.* Trans. John Wilkinson and Purcell Weaver. Notre Dame, IN: University of Notre Dame Press.

Peri, Alessandra. 2001–2002. "Teoria e prassi degli ἐγκώμια ἄδοξα." *Incontri Triestini di Filologia Classica* 1:25–34.

Pernot, Laurent. 1993a. *La rhétorique de l'éloge dans le monde gréco-romain.* Paris: Institut d'Études Augustiniennes.

———. 1993b. "Un rendez-vous manqué." *Rhetorica* 11:421–434.

———. 1997. *Éloges grecs de Rome.* Paris: Les Belles Lettres.

———. 1998. "*Periautologia*: Problèmes et méthodes de l'éloge de soi même dans la tradition éthique et rhétorique gréco-romaine." *Revue des Études Grecques* 111:101–124.

———. 2003. "Grégoire de Nazianze (*Or.* XXXIII, 6–7) et l'éloge rhétorique des cités." *Euphrosyne* 31:271–286.

———. 2005a. "Le lieu du nom (*topos apo tou onomatos*) dans la rhétorique religieuse des Grecs." In *Nommer les dieux: Théonymes, épithètes, épiclèses dans l'Antiquité*, ed. Nicole Belayche et al., 29–39. Turnhout: Brepols.

———. 2005b. *Rhetoric in Antiquity.* Trans. W. E. Higgins. Washington, DC: Catholic University of America Press.

———. 2006. "The Rhetoric of Religion." *Rhetorica* 24:235–254.

———. 2007. "Hymne en vers ou hymne en prose? L'usage de la prose dans l'hymnographie grecque." In Lehmann 2007:169–188.

———. 2008a. "Aelius Aristides and Rome." In *Aelius Aristides between Greece, Rome, and the Gods*, ed. William V. Harris and Brooke Holmes, 175–201. Leiden: Brill.

———. 2008b. "Les faux-semblants de la rhétorique grecque." In *République des lettres, république des arts. Mélanges offerts à Marc Fumaroli, de l'Académie française*, ed. Christian Mouchel and Colette Nativel, 427–450. Geneva: Droz.

———. 2009. "Le acclamazioni: Un nuovo campo di ricerca per la storia della retorica antica." *Atti della Accademia Pontaniana, Napoli*, n.s., 58:177–188.

———. 2010. "Callinicos de Pétra, sophiste et historien." *Revue des Études Grecques* 123:71–90.

———. 2011a. "Elogio retorico e potere politico all'epoca della Seconda Sofistica." In Urso 2011:281–298.

———. 2011b. "Théophraste, un innovateur dans le domaine de la rhétorique." *Comptes Rendus de l'Académie des Inscriptions et Belles-Lettres*: 1277–1306.

Piazza, Francesca. 2008. *La Retorica di Aristotele: Introduzione alla lettura.* Rome: Carocci.

Plöbst, Walter. 1911. *Die Auxesis (Amplificatio): Studien zu ihrer Entwicklung und Anwendung.* Munich: Wolf.

Pont, Anne-Valérie. 2009. "Rituels civiques (*apantēsis* et acclamations) et gouverneurs à l'époque romaine en Asie Mineure." In *Ritual Dynamics and Religious Change in the Roman Empire*, ed. Olivier Hekster, Sebastian Schmidt-Hofner, and Christian Witschel, 185–211. Leiden: Brill.

Pordomingo, Francisca. 2007. "Ejercicios preliminares de la composición retórica y literaria en papiro: El encomio." In *Escuela y literatura en Grecia antigua*, ed. José Antonio Fernández Delgado, Francisca Pordomingo, and Antonio Stramaglia, 405–453. Cassino: Università degli Studi di Cassino.

Poulakos, John. 1995. *Sophistical Rhetoric in Classical Greece.* Columbia: University of South Carolina Press.

Prinz, Karl. 1997. *Epitaphios Logos: Struktur, Funktion und Bedeutung der Bestattungsreden im Athen des 5. und 4. Jahrhunderts.* Frankfurt: Lang.

Rabe, Hugo. 1892–1893. *Syriani in Hermogenem Commentaria.* Leipzig: Teubner.

———. 1931. *Prolegomenon Sylloge.* Leipzig: Teubner.

Race, William H. 1987. "Pindaric Encomium and Isokrates' *Evagoras*." *Transactions and Proceedings of the American Philological Association* 117:131–155.

Rackham, Harris. 1934. *Aristotle: The Nicomachean Ethics.* London: Heinemann; Cambridge, MA: Harvard University Press.

Radermacher, Ludwig. 1951. *Artium scriptores (Reste der voraristotelischen Rhetorik).* Vienna: Rohrer.

Radice, Betty. 1969. *Pliny: Letters and Panegyricus.* London: Heinemann; Cambridge, MA: Harvard University Press.

Rees, Roger. 2002. *Layers of Loyalty in Latin Panegyric: AD 289–307.* Oxford: Oxford University Press.

———. 2007. "Letters of Recommendation and the Rhetoric of Praise." In *Ancient Letters: Classical and Late Antique Epistolography*, ed. Ruth Morello and Andrew D. Morrison, 149–168. Oxford: Oxford University Press.

———, ed. 2012. *Latin Panegyric*. Oxford: Oxford University Press.

Robert, Jeanne, and Louis Robert. 1977. "Bulletin épigraphique 287." *Revue des Études Grecques* 90:364–366.

Robert, Louis. 1938. "Décret de Delphes pour un encomiographe." *Études épigraphiques et philologiques*, 17–30. Paris: Champion.

———. 1948. *Hellenica: Recueil d'épigraphie, de numismatique et d'antiquités grecques*, vol. 4: *Épigrammes du Bas-Empire*. Paris: Maisonneuve.

———. 1970. "Deux concours grecs à Rome." *Comptes Rendus de l'Académie des Inscriptions et Belles-Lettres*: 6–27.

———. 1971. "Rapport sur les travaux de l'École française d'Athènes pendant l'année 1970." *Comptes Rendus de l'Académie des Inscriptions et Belles-Lettres*: 522–539.

———. 1977. "La titulature de Nicée et de Nicomédie: La gloire et la haine." *Harvard Studies in Classical Philology* 81:1–39.

———. 1982. "Une vision de Perpétue martyre à Carthage en 203." *Comptes Rendus de l'Académie des Inscriptions et Belles-Lettres*: 228–276.

———. 1984. "Discours d'ouverture." In *Praktika tou e' diethnous sunedriou Hellēnikēs kai Latinikēs epigraphikēs* 1, 35–45. Athens: Epigraphical Museum.

Roche, Paul A., ed. 2011. *Pliny's Praise: The Panegyricus in the Roman World*. Cambridge: Cambridge University Press.

Romeo, Alessandra. 2004. "Il proemio della *Pharsalia*: Tecnica compositiva e intento encomiastico." *Atti della Accademia Pontaniana*, n.s., 53:319–334.

———. 2012. *Cicerone e l'elogio retorico: Per una lettura del De oratore*. Cosenza: Pellegrini.

Romilly, Jacqueline de. 1975. *Magic and Rhetoric in Ancient Greece*. Cambridge, MA: Harvard University Press.

———. 1992. *The Great Sophists in Periclean Athens*. Trans. Janet Lloyd. Oxford: Clarendon Press.

Rountree, Clarke. 2001. "The (Almost) Blameless Genre of Classical Greek Epideictic." *Rhetorica* 19:293–305.

Rouse, William H. D. 1912. *St. Augustine's Confessions, with an English Translation by William Watts, 1631*. London: Heinemann; Cambridge, MA: Harvard University Press.

Russell, Donald A. 1979. "Rhetors at the Wedding." *Proceedings of the Cambridge Philological Society*, n.s., 25:104–117.

———. 2001. *Quintilian: The Orator's Education*. Cambridge, MA: Harvard University Press.

Russell, Donald A., and Nigel G. Wilson. 1981. *Menander Rhetor*. Oxford: Clarendon Press.

Savon, Hervé. 1980. "La première oraison funèbre de saint Ambroise (*De excessu fratris* I) et les deux sources de la consolation chrétienne." *Revue des Études Latines* 58:370–402.

Schindler, Claudia. 2009. *Per carmina laudes: Untersuchungen zur spätantiken Verspanegyrik von Claudian bis Coripp*. Berlin: De Gruyter.

Schirren, Thomas. 2008. "Der *theôros* als *kritês*: Zum epideiktischen Genos in Arist. *Rhet.* 1, 3." In *Papers on Rhetoric, IX*, ed. Lucia Calboli Montefusco, 197–211. Rome: Herder.

Shackleton Bailey, David R., John T. Ramsey, and Gesine Manuwald. 2009. *Cicero: Philippics 1–6*. Cambridge, MA: Harvard University Press.

Sharpe, Kevin. 1987. *Criticism and Compliment: The Politics of Literature in the England of Charles I*. Cambridge: Cambridge University Press.

Shelton, Jo-Ann. 2013. *The Women of Pliny's Letters*. London: Routledge.

Sideras, Alexander. 2002. *Eine byzantinische Invektive gegen die Verfasser von Grabreden: Ἀνωνύμου μονῳδία εἰς μονῳδοῦντας. Erstmals herausgegeben, übersetzt und kommentiert*. Vienna: Österreichischen Akademie der Wissenschaften.

Slusser, Michael. 1998. *St. Gregory Thaumaturgus: Life and Works*. Washington, DC: Catholic University of America Press.

Smith, Charles F. 1919–1923. *Thucydides: History of the Peloponnesian War*. London: Heinemann; Cambridge, MA: Harvard University Press.

Smith, Christopher, and Ralph Covino, eds. 2010. *Praise and Blame in Roman Republican Rhetoric*. Swansea: Classical Press of Wales.

Soffel, Joachim. 1974. *Die Regeln Menanders für die Leichenrede in ihrer Tradition dargestellt, herausgegeben, übersetzt und kommentiert*. Meisenheim am Glan: Hain.

Spengel, Leonard. 1853–1856. *Rhetores Graeci*. Leipzig: Teubner.

Spina, Luigi. 1999. "Non è difficile fare l'elogio degli Ateniesi ad Atene . . ." In *Papers on Rhetoric, II*, ed. Lucia Calboli Montefusco, 121–132. Bologna: CLUEB.

———. 2000. *La forma breve del dolore: Ricerche sugli epigrammi funerari greci*. Amsterdam: Hakkert.

———. 2001. *L'oratore scriteriato: Per una storia letteraria e politica di Tersite*. Naples: Loffredo.

Stecher, Anton. 1981. *Inschriftliche Grabgedichte auf Krieger und Athleten: Eine Studie zu griechischen Wertprädikationen*. Innsbruck: Wagner.

Stock, Aloysius. 1911. *De prolaliarum usu rhetorico*. Königsberg: Hartung.

Strauss, Leo. 1952. *Persecution and the Art of Writing*. Glencoe, IL: Free Press.

Sullivan, Dale L. 1993. "The Ethos of Epideictic Encounter." *Philosophy and Rhetoric* 26:113–133.

Sutton, Edward W., and Harris Rackham. 1942. *Cicero: De Oratore, Books I, II*. London: Heinemann; Cambridge, MA: Harvard University Press.

Thorpe, M. Elizabeth. 2014. "'Under God': An Epideictic Weapon in the Fight against Communism." In *Re/Framing Identifications*, ed. Michelle Ballif, 28–40. Long Grove, IL: Waveland.

Tsitsiridis, Stavros. 1998. *Platons Menexenos*. Leipzig: Teubner.

Ueding, Gert, ed. 1992–2012. *Historisches Wörterbuch der Rhetorik*. Tübingen: Niemeyer; Berlin: De Gruyter.

Urso, Gianpaolo, ed. 2011. *Dicere laudes: Elogio, comunicazione, creazione del consenso*. Pisa: ETS.

Usener, Hermann, and Ludwig Radermacher. 1899–1929. *Dionysii Halicarnasei quae extant 5–6: Opuscula*. Leipzig: Teubner.

Valiavitcharska, Vessela. 2006. "Correct *Logos* and Truth in Gorgias' *Encomium of Helen*." *Rhetorica* 24:147–161.

Vallozza, Maddalena. 1989. "Il motivo dell'invidia in Pindaro." *Quaderni Urbinati di Cultura Classica* 60:13–30.

———. 2001. "Καιρός nella teoria del discorso di lode." *Daidalos* 3:249–258.

Van der Poel, Marc. 1996. "*Paradoxon* et *adoxon* chez Ménandre le Rhéteur et chez les humanistes du début du XVIe siècle." In *Le paradoxe en linguistique et en littérature*, ed. Ronald Landheer and Paul J. Smith, 199–220. Geneva: Droz.

Velardi, Roberto. 1991. "Le origini dell'inno in prosa tra V e IV secolo a.C.: Menandro Retore e Platone." *AION Sezione filologico-letteraria* 13:205–231.

Vérilhac, Anne-Marie. 1978–1982. *Παῖδες ἄωροι. Poésie funéraire*. Athens: Akadēmia Athēnōn.

Vickers, Brian. 1982–1983. "Epideictic and Epic in the Renaissance." *New Literary History* 14:497–537.

———. 1983. "Epideictic Rhetoric in Galileo's *Dialogo*." *Annali dell'Istituto e Museo di Storia della Scienza di Firenze* 8:69–102.

Viljamaa, Toivo. 1968. *Studies in Greek Encomiastic Poetry of the Early Byzantine Period*. Helsinki: Societas Scientiarum Fennica.

Vix, Jean-Luc. 2010. *L'enseignement de la rhétorique au IIe siècle ap. J.-C. à travers les discours 30–34 d'Aelius Aristide*. Turnhout: Brepols.

Walker, Jeffrey. 2000. *Rhetoric and Poetics in Antiquity*. Oxford: Oxford University Press.

———. 2004. "These Things I Have Not Betrayed: Michael Psellos' Encomium of His Mother as a Defense of Rhetoric." *Rhetorica* 22:49–101.

———. 2011. *The Genuine Teachers of This Art: Rhetorical Education in Antiquity.* Columbia: University of South Carolina Press.

Wallace-Hadrill, Andrew. 1981. "The Emperor and His Virtues." *Historia* 30:298–323.

Walz, Christian. 1832–1836. *Rhetores Graeci.* Stuttgart: Cotta.

Walzer, Arthur E. 2013. "*Parrēsia*, Foucault, and the Classical Rhetorical Tradition." *Rhetoric Society Quarterly* 43:1–21.

Webb, Ruth. 2003. "Praise and Persuasion: Argumentation and Audience Response in Epideictic Oratory." In *Rhetoric in Byzantium*, ed. Elizabeth Jeffreys, 127–135. Aldershot: Ashgate.

———. 2009. *Ekphrasis, Imagination, and Persuasion in Ancient Rhetorical Theory and Practice.* Burlington, VT: Ashgate.

Whitby, Mary, ed. 1998. *The Propaganda of Power: The Role of Panegyric in Late Antiquity.* Leiden: Brill.

Whitmarsh, Tim. 2001. *Greek Literature and the Roman Empire: The Politics of Imitation.* Oxford: Oxford University Press.

———. 2005. *The Second Sophistic.* Greece and Rome: New Surveys in the Classics 35. Cambridge: Cambridge University Press.

Woods, Marjorie C. 2009. "The Classroom as Courtroom: Cicero's Attributes of Persons and the Interpretation of Classical Literary Characters in the Renaissance." In *Ciceroniana: Atti del XIII Colloquium Tullianum*, 203–215. Rome: Centro di Studi Ciceroniani.

Wörrle, Michael. 1988. *Stadt und Fest im kaiserzeitlichen Kleinasien: Studien zu einer agonistischen Stiftung aus Oinoanda.* Munich: Beck.

———. 1995. "Vom tugendsamen Jüngling zum 'gestreßten' Euergeten: Überlegungen zum Bürgerbild hellenisticher Ehrendekrete." In *Stadtbild und Bürgerbild im Hellenismus*, ed. Michael Wörrle and Paul Zanker, 241–250. Munich: Beck.

Worthington, Ian, ed. 2007. *A Companion to Greek Rhetoric.* Oxford: Blackwell.

Wright, Wilmer C. 1921. *Philostratus and Eunapius: The Lives of the Sophists.* London: Heinemann; Cambridge, MA: Harvard University Press.

Wuellner, Wilhelm. 1979. "Greek Rhetoric and Pauline Argumentation." In *Early Christian Literature and the Classical Intellectual Tradition: In honorem Robert M. Grant*, ed. William R. Schoedel and Robert L. Wilken, 177–188. Paris: Beauchesne.

Yunis, Harvey. 2011. *Plato: Phaedrus.* Cambridge: Cambridge University Press.

Zagagi, Netta. 1985. "Helen of Troy: Encomium and Apology." *Wiener Studien* 98:63–88.

Zarini, Vincent. 2005. "Le problème de l'éloge dans la *Vita Martini* de Sulpice Sévère." *Vita Latina* 172:130–144.

Ziegler, Konrat. 1949. "Panegyrikos." *Paulys Real-Encyclopädie der klassischen Altertumswissenschaft* 18:559–581.

Zoberman, Pierre. 1991. *Les Panégyriques du Roi prononcés dans l'Académie française*. Paris: Presses de l'Université Paris–Sorbonne.

———. 1998. *Les cérémonies de la parole: L'éloquence d'apparat en France dans le dernier quart du XVIIe siècle*. Paris: Champion.

INDEX

www.ingramcontent.com/pod-product-compliance
Lightning Source LLC
LaVergne TN
LVHW090024310826
846742LV00010B/26
* 9 7 8 1 4 7 7 3 1 1 3 3 2 *